ADHOCRACY

THE

POWER

TO

CHANGE

BOOKS
BY
ROBERT H.
WATERMAN JR.

THE RENEWAL FACTOR:
HOW THE BEST GET AND KEEP THE COMPETITIVE EDGE

IN SEARCH OF EXCELLENCE:
LESSONS FROM AMERICA'S BEST-RUN COMPANIES
(coauthor)

ADHOCRACY

THE
POWER
TO
CHANGE

BY ROBERT H. WATERMAN JR.

WHITTLE DIRECT BOOKS

Photographs by Michele Clement, with the following exceptions: Frederick Taylor, The Bettmann
Archive, page 9; Ken Derr provided by Chevron Corporation, page 17; Lewis Veraldi
provided by Ford Motor Company, page 58.

Library of Congress Catalog Card Number: 89-52041
Waterman, Robert H.
Adhocracy: The Power to Change
ISBN 0-9624745-1-7
ISSN 1046-364X

The Larger Agenda Series

The Larger Agenda Series presents original short books by distinguished authors on subjects of importance to managers and policymakers in business and the public sector.

The series is edited and published by Whittle Communications L.P., an independent publishing company. A new book appears approximately every other month. The series reflects a broad spectrum of responsible opinions. In each book the opinions expressed are those of the author, not the publisher or the advertiser.

I welcome your comments on this unique endeavor.

William S. Rukeyser
Editor in Chief

CONTENTS

11:49 PM, Memphis, Tennessee. Packages sorted at main hub.

In the early '70s, Federal Express pioneered overnight air express in the U.S. Today, Federal Express offers reliable air express delivery worldwide.

THE POWER OF ADHOCRACY

L ee Gammill beams as he tells his story. "In two days, we designed the product that absolutely blew the industry apart. We had an *80 percent* increase in volume within one year. We're a big company—even an 8 percent increase would have been great."

Frozen pizzas? Personal computers? Post-it notes? Not at all. Gammill is an executive vice-president of New York Life Insurance Company. The product he's describing is a radically redesigned whole life policy. In just two years the product boosted New York Life's market share by two percentage points, an astonishing increase in an industry that most of us think of as huge, entrenched, and stagnant.

In the spring of 1986 Gammill had been offered a promotion to senior vice-president. Management felt that the company had lost touch with the marketplace. Sparking any enthusiasm in the New York Life sales organization was getting tough, let alone igniting the top agents, who were clearly disenchanted with what the company had to offer. Gammill's new assignment would be to redesign the core product line, repackage it, and make it sell.

He agonized over the decision. Gammill had begun his career in 1957 as an agent for New York Life and had worked his way up through the ranks. He was now in charge of the San Francisco office, and that was nice duty. Taking the new job would mean moving to New York. But Gammill liked the challenge. He accepted—and made a personal vow never

Lee Gammill of New York Life Insurance Company cut across traditional bureaucratic boundaries to form an ad hoc team that increased sales by 80 percent in one year.

to design any product without bringing in the agents. He felt strongly that the people who sold the company's products should help make design decisions.

"To my knowledge, this had never been done before," he says. "Typically, actuaries would design products. They got a little input on customers from home-office sales-promotion guys, who told the actuaries what they thought the field would want." That problem is hardly unique to the insurance industry. Companies commonly design products with little or no input from salespeople or customers.

"I brought in six top sales guys—all different ages and from different parts of the country, all fairly outspoken," Gammill says. "I put them in a room with four designers, three actuaries, a competition specialist, a couple of technicians, and a service person. And I said, 'Now we're going to design a term policy, a whole life policy, and any other product we can.'

"The actuaries started to present a new term policy based on some preliminary studies they'd done. As they went along, it became clear that the proposal wasn't any good. The agents kept telling them that. For about an hour, I just kept quiet while the actuaries defended their baby. At the end I said, 'Stop! Don't try to jam anything down anybody's throat. These agents have just told you that it's a lousy product. They won't sell it. I want you to hear what *will* sell and then find some common ground. We're not leaving this room until we're done.'

"It took two days. We didn't let anybody out of that damned room, and we designed the product of a lifetime."

The company's new whole life policy was unconventional, to say the least. A high-dividend product, it offered the policyholder more protection than before without costing a fortune in premiums. The trade-off was less cash value down the road. The product solved two problems that, until then, had the industry stumped: customers were growing more financially astute, and interest rates were going through the roof. This pernicious pair had devastated the traditional whole life concept. The new approach was a little like term insurance without the spiraling premium hikes. Agents and their customers loved it.

Gammill shows us just how responsive an organization can be when it breaks with tradition, cuts across old boundaries, and pulls the right group of people together to go after an opportunity. The New York Life story is a fine example of what I call adhocracy. Apples from one department, oranges from another, coming together to find solutions to common problems. Broadly defined, adhocracy is any organizational form that challenges the bureaucracy in order to embrace the new. Like Gammill's "17 guys in a room," it transcends organizational charts, functions, job descriptions. Adhocracy can be as mundane as a get-together over coffee, a manager and his assistant trying to figure out how to keep the restrooms in paper towels. It can be as swashbuckling as Steven Jobs and his loyal band at Apple Computer Inc. marching off to a separate building, hoisting a skull and crossbones, and developing the Macintosh.

Why manage adhocracy? Simply put, ad hoc organizational forms are *the* most powerful tools we have for effecting change. The clout of even the most aggressive chief executive pales by comparison—if adhocracy is well run. In many companies today one measure of a manager's effectiveness is his track record in leading teams and task forces. A manager who can launch a task force, keep it on track, and get results without uprooting sound bureaucratic infrastructure—that is a manager with a bright future. Unfortunately, managing that way requires a whole set of skills that can't be acquired through formal training. In business schools, adhocracy has been all but ignored.

LESSONS FROM
THE CHANGEMASTERS

This book is about adhocracy at its best. I've focused on the most common, sturdy, and visible ad hoc form: the project team, or task force. I've drawn lessons from a handful of companies that successfully manage adhocracy. Some are clients; others are companies I've admired from afar. The inspiration for this book comes from people like Lee Gammill who have learned through trial and error how to change their organizations fast and with good effect. These executives are the rising stars of corporate America. They have much to teach.

Why am I such a believer in the power of well-managed adhocracy? Consider the difficulty America and its institutions seem to have coping with change. We think of the main structure of any organization as bureaucracy, applying that word in its most congenial sense. Bureaucracy gets us through the day; it deals efficiently with everyday problems. The trouble is, change ignores conventional bureaucratic lines. The real action in organizations occurs outside "the proper channels." We all know this, yet we act as if we don't. We try to use the bureaucracy to cope with change. It's the wrong approach.

I'm amazed and dismayed at our seeming hamhandedness in a global economy—especially in competing with Japan, where I've lived and worked. As author James Fallows says, we cannot be like the Japanese any more than they can be like us. But I believe we can learn from them, just as they went to school on us. One of Japan's great competitive strengths is that its people put less faith in bureaucracy and more in adhocracy as a normal way of managing. They manage adhocracy; we don't.

Another source of wonder is the booming consulting business—the business that will rent you an ad hoc team. Clearly I'm a believer in outside help; I have a career invested in it. What puzzles me is why executives so willingly shell out several hundred thousand dollars a month for projects that their own managers ought to be able to handle. "I don't know what we've spent on management-consulting contracts," laments Lee Gammill, "but the figure is huge." He could be speaking for hundreds of executives when he describes a recent consulting project: "We studied every department. The work was good. But we got buried in tomes and paper. We did nothing with any of that stuff."

Most executives I talk with share Gammill's view. I hear praise for the consultants' expertise and brainpower, dismay at the great expense and disappointing results, and ire that more cannot be done by managers within. As I look back on my own career, I find that one factor sets the most successful projects apart: during the course of the project, the client learned to manage adhocracy.

The concept of adhocracy is not new. In the mid-1960s, management theorist Warren Bennis argued the need for "adaptive, problem-solving, temporary systems of diverse specialists linked together...in an organic flux." Alvin Toffler talked about ad hoc forms in his book *Future Shock*. But nobody ever really fleshed out the idea, applied it to the business world, sought out success stories, or outlined their common themes.

American business had it easy from the end of World War II until the onslaught of global competition. There was enough slack in the system to stick to the old ways and more or less keep up. Today we don't have that luxury. My view is that we either learn to manage adhocracy or continue our slide toward mediocrity.

The well-run ad hoc team has several attributes that make it the ideal organization for change. First, like change itself, it cuts across conventional lines and boundaries. "The world is getting so complex that almost anything that you do is a wheel with a spoke that reaches out into all the other functional areas," says Thomas Tusher, president of Levi Strauss & Company, who has managed, led, and participated in many ad hoc teams throughout his career. "The task force allows us to bring those different disciplines together. On big issues, if one function does what is best for them, it might not be best for the organization."

Second, the well-run project team is designed to effect change. It solves one of the most common management problems of the last 20 years: great strategy, lousy implementation. Well-managed adhocracy requires the broad participation that is so vital to implementation. When Lee Gammill adjourned his closed-door design meeting, the work of the task force had just begun. The technicians were sent off to central processing to hook up a network of personal computers—one for each agent. The agents joined the actuaries in designing software that would enable them to spew out elaborate "what if" scenarios for prospective customers. The marketing people packaged videotapes of top agents describing

> **My view is that we either learn to manage adhocracy or continue our slide toward mediocrity.**

3:36 PM, Geneva, Switzerland. Overseas shipment delivered to its final destination.

With 30 million international express deliveries under our belt,
Federal Express provides unmatched experience and expertise in dutiable
and document shipments overseas.

the virtues of the whole life product. "We knew that the only way this thing was going to work," says Gammill, "was if we got everybody in the company involved."

Third, the well-run team mounts a frontal attack on everyone's pet nemesis—lack of communication. With widespread involvement comes deep and broad understanding of decisions made along the way. "Task force members eventually become proponents," says Levi's Tusher. "They tell others in their organization what was agreed on and why, and in doing so ensure that there is smooth execution or implementation."

This model of change presents a diametric contrast to our bureaucratic heritage—the pyramid style of management, in which orders are handed down from the top. We value crisp decisions and clear direction, even though my experience has shown that managers who provide them (except in crisis situations) seem to produce little but resistance down the line.

Finally, the best thinking very often results from a team effort. With few exceptions, repeated research has established that groups are usually better than individuals at solving new and unfamiliar problems in areas where no one in the company is an expert.

A forceful example is an exercise called the Desert Survival Situation. Participants are told that they have just crash-landed in a small plane in the middle of the Sonora Desert. They are uninjured, but the pilot and copilot have been killed, and the aircraft has burned. A few items—maps, clothing, tools, and so on—have been recovered from the wreckage. The participants are asked to rank each item in order of its importance to their survival and to come up with their own survival plan. Then groups of four to six people are given about an hour to develop a team solution. Almost without exception, the teams outperform any individual.

Joel Peterson, managing partner at Trammell Crow Company, the Dallas-based commercial real estate developer, is clearly a proponent of this concept. Faced with the double whammy of radically different real estate tax policies and a depression in the oil patch, Peterson decided to enlist the aid of his people in helping him get the company back on track. He created an adhocracy—four project teams that he assigned to study and make recommendations on four critical areas.

"It's been a tough lesson for me," Peterson admits. "I'm wired to think that I can figure these things out by myself. But the fact is, I'm not an expert in the emerging market environment. There is no expert. Nobody has seen it before. So the collective wisdom of the group is one of the strongest advantages we have."

If adhocracy seems so right—if Gammill, Tusher, and Peterson use it with such effect—then most people may assume that every manager is facile in managing adhocracy. My experience says the reverse is true.

BREAKING THE HABIT

Most of us are like the characters in Ibsen's play *Ghosts*. We're controlled by ideas and norms that have outlived their usefulness, that are only ghosts but have as much influence on our behavior as they would if they were alive. The ideas of men like Henry Ford, Frederick Taylor, and Max Weber—these are the ghosts that haunt our halls of management.

Frederick Taylor started our limited way of thinking about management with the time-and-motion studies he began in 1881.

People at Ford Motor Company tell the story of a worker whose job was to lift heavy transmissions. One day he stopped his boss in the hallway and said, "I've got an idea that might improve this operation." The foreman looked at him in disbelief. "Forget that stuff," he finally snarled. "We didn't hire you to think."

That was Ford in the 1950s—still yoked to the brilliant but outdated ideas of its founder. "The old system thought of the worker as a single-purpose machine tool," says CEO Donald Petersen. That old system hung on until the 1980s. What Ford referred to as its chimneys of power—the boundaries between functions—was so entrenched that when the company finally inaugurated sweeping changes, it had to bring in facilitators to teach executives how to improve communication between divisions.

If one were to fix a starting point for the limited way we think about management, it might be 1881. That's when Frederick Taylor began his time-and-motion studies. Working at Midvale Steel Company in Philadelphia, armed with a stopwatch, Taylor closely observed plant workers, his goal being to eliminate wasted time and motion. His recommendations were disarmingly simple: companies could and should program workers and the repetitive work they do. Taylor saw workers as robots.

Around the turn of this century, the German sociologist Max Weber conceived the bureaucracy in part to redress corrupt and unjust management practices dating back to the early days of the Industrial Revolution. Henry Ford's Model T assembly line was the perfect synthesis of Weber's idea of management and Taylor's view of labor. Managers of manufacturing plants during and after World War II, who began using the terms *staff*, *line*, and especially *chain of command*, further reinforced the idea of the organization as a pyramid, hierarchy, and bureaucracy.

These outdated ideas have led to lack of experience and training in the kinds of tasks that cut across conventional boundaries, yet they still shape American organizations. The problem is habit. We've spent more than a century developing and polishing a management paradigm that resists change. As much as we talk about the horrors of bureaucracy, as much as we poke fun at red tape, as much as we rail at the slowness of officialdom, we still try to get most things done through the same tired, bureaucratic means.

Habit haunts us even when we ought to know better. Stress—the kind produced by rapid change—seems to make us revert to mindless, programmed behavior. Maybe we're just fearful of change and failure, for even when we know a situation cries out for adhocracy, we often choose the old, familiar path.

Many habits are useful; we wouldn't be able to get through the day without them. Habit in general is comforting. But how do we break those old habits that have outlived their usefulness? Social scientists have some suggestions that apply just as well to management inertia as to any other stubborn habit. First, make a public commitment to change. Second, take at least one small step in the new direction as soon as possible. Third, go cold turkey; no lapses allowed. Finally, build in tremendous positive reinforcement for the new behavior, and don't slow down long enough to let old habits sneak back.

Without reading the prescription, Lee Gammill followed it to the letter. He told anyone within earshot about his vow never to design a product without input from agents. He assembled his task force, designed his product, and mounted his sales campaign without breaking stride. He poured on the praise as sales climbed. Now, three years later, adhocracy has successfully challenged bureaucratic hegemony as the force to be reckoned with at New York Life.

RUN TO DAYLIGHT

In the 1960s the Green Bay Packers, led by Coach Vince Lombardi, were invincible. Their passing game was strong. Their running game was superb. Every player had a carefully prescribed role, an opponent to block, a pattern to run. But one of the coach's most valuable rules never made it into the playbook. It was the command he barked out from the sidelines every time one of his backs got the ball and turned upfield: Run to daylight. Do what it takes to take advantage of an opportunity. Don't throw away the playbook, but don't blindly follow the rules if common sense tells you they won't work.

Run to daylight. Adhocracy isn't business as usual. The work defines the leading edge. It is adventure capital and ought to feel that way. Whether the immediate goal is to design a new product, pull together divisions working at cross-purposes, or save a company in crisis, the mood should be one of excitement, experimentation, and urgency.

I've seen adhocracy at its best and worst. Some organizations are bombarded with task forces—few of them effective but all still in place. Some organizations never use project teams on important management issues. Some companies are wonderful at using project teams to develop products or construct buildings, but they can't transfer that skill to other issues. Some managers try to avoid adhocracy altogether by handing over "ownership" of crucial problems to consultants with little or no stake in the outcome. Some organizations, especially small ones, are adhocracies only. That's fine when they're small. But as they grow, they're so afraid of bigness that they do everything ad hoc, becoming just as rigid as the most fossilized bureaucracy.

Some people would argue that bureaucracy should be destroyed. I don't buy that. The issue is not adhocracy versus bureaucracy. Both are necessary. Teams are temporary, but adhocracy is permanent, just like bureaucracy. Any manager worth his salt will be proficient in working with both. Management theorist Peter Drucker predicted the duality in the early 1970s: "Every business—and every other institution—has been using teams all along for ad hoc, nonrecurrent tasks. But we have only recently recognized what our nomadic ice age ancestors knew: the team is also a principle for permanent structural design."

Today's companies need, but seldom have, the ability to move seamlessly from bureaucracy to adhocracy and back again. Today's managers need, but seldom have, the skill and security to leave their posts for a while and become effective members of project teams. But without that ability, companies and people go on making the same old mistakes. They do not learn. This is the Achilles' heel of corporate America.

3:28 AM, Memphis, Tennessee. Customer service agents field calls.

Questions about overseas delivery? Talk to a specially trained international expert toll-free. 24 hours a day. 365 days a year.

1:30 PM, Milano, Italy. Courier making deliveries.

The Federal Express worldwide network provides on-time delivery of your packages in over 118 countries on six continents.

THE RIGHT START

Just as the Green Bay Packers dominated football in the 1960s, the San Francisco 49ers dominated in the 1980s. Like Vince Lombardi, Bill Walsh was the coach of a decade. Among Walsh's coaching idiosyncrasies was this: He mapped out the first 20 or so offensive plays before every game. The reason was simple. Walsh wanted extra assurance that the 49ers were off to the right start. Repeated practice of those plays meant confidence going into the game, fine execution from the outset, frequent first-quarter scores, and momentum that was hard to stop.

The right start is even more crucial for adhocracy. A well-conceived team can survive dismal management and still turn out a workmanlike product. A poorly launched team can run like an executive's Rolex and still not get the job done.

CLEAR AND VISIBLE
EXECUTIVE SUPPORT

Phillip Williams, a vice-chairman of the Times Mirror Company, is a big believer in adhocracy. He expresses very well what I consider to be the number-one rule of launching a team: "If you don't have the clear support and blessing of the senior management, a task force won't work. People will not perceive it as being important. The effort won't be credible." To work successfully, adhocracy has to have conspicuous, overt, palpable, obvious-to-everyone support from the top. If a project is important enough, that support has to come from the chief executive.

My first encounter with this fact of life in adhocracy was on a team working with Ronald Reagan's administration when he was California's governor. Reagan had set up two task forces—one on welfare reform, the other on education. The first produced fairly respectable results. The second, in my view, failed. Why the difference? For whatever reasons, signs of Reagan's interest in the first project were everywhere. He was always available to the head of the welfare team, even though that individual was several layers down in the state bureaucracy. If the team needed Reagan's support in battling the state legislature, that support was there. In contrast, if Reagan felt strongly about education, his interest didn't show.

Chevron Corporation is one of the best examples of a company skilled at using project teams. The company was already an oil-industry giant when, in 1984, it acquired Gulf Corporation for $13.2 billion, overnight becoming America's 11th-largest publicly held industrial corporation. When corporate raider T. Boone Pickens put the Gulf takeover deal into play, Chevron was at first a reluctant suitor, daunted by the size of the deal (at the time the biggest in corporate history). But the more Chevron's managers studied the deal, the more they realized the fit was as near perfect as they would find. They might never see a better opportunity.

I was intrigued by the sheer speed of the transaction and subsequent merger. George Keller, then Chevron's chief executive, made his complete presentation to the Gulf board from one 3- by 5-inch scrap of paper on which he had written out notes the night before. Rod Willoughby, Chevron's treasurer, got on the phone to his banking contacts around the world, moving from time zone to time zone—Tokyo, Frankfurt, Zurich, Paris, London, New York. Within 24 hours Willoughby had lined up the unprecedented financing needed to complete the transaction. The usual armies of lawyers and investment bankers were never mustered.

Having completed the transaction on paper, Chevron and Gulf managers didn't miss a beat in carrying out the merger.

Chief executive Ken Derr orchestrated the efforts of 37 project teams to carry out Chevron's merger with Gulf, one of the largest deals in corporate history.

Working closely with their counterparts at Gulf, Chevron managers put together no fewer than 37 task forces to merge the best parts from both companies. Teams stormed every nook and cranny of both organizations: exploration, drilling, production, refining, marketing, finance, data processing—the list goes on.

Throughout, not only did the teams have a large slice of Keller's time and attention, but Ken Derr—then president of Chevron USA, who later took Keller's place as chief executive—was pulled from his job to spend full time, and then some, orchestrating all the teams' efforts.

In retrospect, Chevron's efficient execution of both the deal and the merger is not surprising. Like Walsh's 49ers, the company was well rehearsed. Vice-chairman Jim Sullivan says he can't think of a time when Chevron did not operate as both bureaucracy and adhocracy. His first encounter with Chevron's version of adhocracy occurred when he was a young line manager. A senior officer whom he'd never met before wandered into his office. The man was a member of a team studying some organizational issues, and he wanted Sullivan's views. Since then Sullivan has participated in or run more project teams than he can remember. During the Chevron-Gulf transition, he helped Derr coordinate the efforts of the 37 teams. These days he commissions teams and, as one of the top three people at Chevron, he's a busy guy.

Sullivan makes sure, however, that he spends enough time with the teams he sponsors. "People on those teams should be stepping high," he says. He ensures that they do so by showing again and again that he's involved, interested, and taking their efforts seriously.

Top management support not only gives a project credibility; it's also an important perk. Ad hoc work is difficult and stressful for most people. It is highly unstructured—no matter how careful the planning, projects take unpredictable twists and turns. And the work takes people away from home; meetings and interviews require travel. It also requires a mental shift; team members may well be cut loose for a while from their normal box on the organizational chart.

To make matters worse, reward systems in most companies—salaries, bonuses, options—are typically tied to one's box in the bureaucracy. They don't usually compensate for the large hunks of time and extra effort that people must commit to projects outside established channels. People will not spend the time, take the work seriously, or feel good about what they're doing unless top executives are involved and perceived as sharing the sense that the project is a top priority.

Frequent interaction with upper management has another important benefit: it keeps teams on track. On a typical project, one issue leads to another, that one to a third, and so on. Tangents trap project teams. No matter how objective, honest, and focused teams try to be, they do not have top management's perspective. Left alone for long periods, there-fore, teams can produce wonderful reports that get shot down with a statement like "The work seems good, but you for-got to take our new employee-involvement program into account."

Many companies use steering committees to keep teams focused. Chevron's steering committees are composed of five to seven executives representing the various divisions that will be affected by the outcome of the teams' work. Chosen by the executive sponsoring the project, in collaboration with his or her peers and sometimes the chief executive, committee members are required to meet bimonthly or quarterly, their main objective being to see that team efforts stay in sync with larger corporate goals. In my view, the most important work of the steering committee is simply to keep top management visibly involved.

Nothing destroys morale faster than managers setting up project teams and not giving them proper attention. Executives often do this to buy time on thorny problems. "We're studying the issue," they say. What they really mean is, "If we wait awhile, maybe the issue will go away."

I've been guilty of this myself, as my staff reminds me with annoying regularity. Their favorite example goes back to when I was a senior partner at McKinsey & Company's San Francisco office. Our lease was expiring, and the proposed new rate would have increased our overhead by more than one million bucks annually. Clearly, we would have to move.

Nothing destroys morale faster than managers setting up project teams and not giving them proper attention.

Since everyone in the office would be affected, we solicited everyone's help in finding new quarters. We set up teams to study various locations and options. Though nobody relished the idea of moving, the teams did their homework and came up with some fine alternatives. Meanwhile, the real estate market in San Francisco unexpectedly softened, and we found that we could negotiate a very favorable lease and stay right where we were.

The partners were delighted, but we made the mistake of relying on word of mouth and never got back to the teams to tell them why, after all the sound and fury, we were not moving. They assumed that we had not been serious about moving in the first place. Our intent had been to build morale by involving everyone in a tough issue. But because we didn't stay involved with the teams throughout the problem-solving process, our credibility withered.

Top management's commitment must be real, begin when the project begins, and must continue throughout the project no matter what the outcome. Doing otherwise doesn't just neuter a task force; it badly undermines management's credibility.

THE BULLETIN-BOARD TEST

Project teams conduct some of the most important work in organizations, so the best people ought to participate. Too often, however, people with time on their hands are the ones who get put on teams. The reason they aren't busy is that they aren't that good.

"We spent a lot of time trying to make sure we picked the right people as team leaders," says Chevron's Ken Derr. "We asked ourselves, 'Will they be respected? How will they deal with others?'" Jim Sullivan calls his system of selecting a team the bulletin-board test. He explains: "Can we put the team's mission, the team leader, and the team members on the bulletin board? Will our people acknowledge that we picked the right team for that problem?"

Failure to find the right leader is reason enough not to proceed, he adds. During the merger, Chevron opted to delay launching a few teams because the obvious leaders wouldn't

1:12 AM, Memphis, Tennessee. Clearing customs at main hub.

Sending a package to or from a foreign land? Federal Express knows the customs—so your package moves swiftly and is delivered on time.

2:45 PM, Hong Kong. Shipments arriving.

Every business day, Federal Express flies nearly 400,000 miles and drives
1.5 million miles to deliver packages throughout the world.

have passed the bulletin-board test. Management knew that if it picked the wrong leaders it would get silly answers or biased results. Most people have fairly vague answers about what constitutes a good team member. The people I questioned were just about as clear as the three bears discussing porridge. Team leaders and members should be neither overbearing nor meek. In other words, just right.

A widespread problem in leadership today—yet another hand-me-down from those bureaucratic ghosts—is a pushy, controlling, directive management style. Such an approach stifles lower-level people in most bureaucracies and is a death sentence for adhocracy.

"I think the best task force tends to be one that does not have a strong [bossy] leader," says Levi's Tom Tusher. "Rather, a task force needs someone to really just keep them on schedule, and who has the skills to say, 'I think we've covered that long enough; let's do it.' Or, 'We've had a lot of dialogue, now I am going to go around the table. Give me your summary position.' Not stating for them what the answers are, but keeping the process flowing."

Bill Crain, Chevron's vice-president of domestic oil and gas, seems to agree. "I've been in some groups where one person wants to dominate, do everything, do all the talking," he says. "That's an impediment. I try to get a group of people that will share ideas and engage in good, healthy debate."

The task force leader emphatically should not be the expert in the area being studied or a member of the top executive ranks. Groups tend to defer to the person with the expertise or the person with power. This defeats the whole purpose of adhocracy. By definition, you are covering ground where nobody's expertise or experience is likely to be much help. You're seeking change. If the senior vice-president of marketing is put in charge of a task force on marketing, you're not likely to get much more than his biased views, better supported and articulated. The bureaucracy dressed in ad hoc clothing is still the bureaucracy.

Process skills, therefore, are as important as knowledge of the problem under scrutiny. These skills sound simple: running a good meeting, setting schedules, keeping things on

> **The bureaucracy dressed in ad hoc clothing is still the bureaucracy.**

track, ensuring that work gets done between meetings, getting input from the whole team (rather than a few dominant members), and listening. But team leaders often lack those skills, or maybe they just forget them the moment they're put on a task force.

The best task force leaders are fun to be with and are genuinely liked by team members. Though the fun factor may be dismissed as frivolous by management theorists, my experience tells me that it's critical. I've heard too many team members gripe that their leaders were inaccessible, and I've seen too many team members miss meetings, claiming that other work is more urgent—because in fact the team leader doesn't enjoy and respect his team, or vice versa. They don't have fun on what ought to be exciting work; instead, they avoid each other.

One final point: Adhocracy is an excellent training ground for future executives. "Pick some of your rising superstars who need more companywide exposure and experience," says Tusher. "Project teams are a good way to make sure that some of your better people—ones who have some shortcomings in interpersonal skills or dealing with people across the organization—get a chance to overcome those weaknesses." Make service in adhocracy an honor. That's the way to get the best people.

TOO MANY COOKS...

Teams should be big enough to represent all parts of the bureaucracy that will be affected by their work, yet small enough to get the job done efficiently. Anyone who has sat through a meeting with too many participants with seemingly endless opportunities for putting in their two cents' worth, can appreciate the problem of unwieldy teams. At the same time, many projects founder on shallow representation.

How do you manage the balancing act? The simple answer is to break big teams into small ones with separate roles. I've found that teams of only two people can be very effective—if the two are working full time on the project. I can remember cases in which the team consisted of one full-timer, a number of part-timers, and a part-time team leader. That never worked. Looking back on my 25 years in consulting, it seems to me that the best teams numbered three to seven full-timers.

Team composition is as important as team size. The general rule is to match the team to the issue. Pick team members who collectively reflect the breadth, nature, and complexity of the problem. At Syntex Corporation, the billion-dollar-a-year pharmaceutical company, managers have found that taking diagonal slices from the company, consisting of people from various disciplines, works best. For many years, Syntex has used task forces to find answers to various human-resource problems: how to improve reward systems, foster teamwork, devise profit-sharing schemes, and so on. Team members would come from every conceivable level in the organization. An executive vice-president from, say, manufacturing. A middle manager from research. A salesman. A secretary. The team in total would be a two-dimensional cross section of the company—one reflecting the functions, and the other reflecting the levels.

Levi Strauss also uses the diagonal-slice method. When the company put together a task force to build an integrated database system, it recruited people from all over the company for their input. "We brought in a representative from each division—systems, operations, finance, and so on—who understood thoroughly how his division would interface with the new system," says Tusher. "Together, the representatives can get all the issues on the table, understand the trade-offs, and finally agree on a strategy that is right."

The diagonal slice works well for two reasons. The executives are just not in the same world as people down the line, yet only the executives can effect change. The reverse is also true: people down the line don't have much perspective beyond their own levels.

Adhocracy needs resources to get the job done properly. That sounds like a platitude, but teams very often fail simply because they're resource-poor. Besides talent, which we've discussed, adhocracy needs money and time resources. The bureaucracy usually determines how people get measured and compensated. Lean is especially mean in today's takeover climate. When an important issue cries out for financial support, its sponsor, and the people who are asked to contribute team members, simply may not have the budget for it.

Even if the budget does exist, team members often don't put enough time into the effort. This reflects a what-gets-measured-gets-done attitude. People are usually measured only by the standards set for their jobs in the bureaucracy. They don't get paid, rewarded, or recognized for contributions to ad hoc efforts. I strongly believe that for the best results companies should devote the resources necessary to put core team members to work full time on the project.

Most of the real work on task forces—interviewing, fact-gathering, analyzing, testing possible solutions—gets done between meetings. Time has to be allowed for that. Meetings are seductively visible. They seem to define adhocracy, but they are only a way of keeping things on schedule. A common pattern that defeats adhocracy is regular attendance and lively discussion at meetings—the appearance of progress—but no real headway. The project peters out because nobody works between meetings.

Hence the argument for full time. If the core team knows that its only job for a while is the project team, there is no alternative but to get the work of adhocracy done.

Chevron often uses full-timers, even though it labels participation part-time. "We did not replace employees in whatever job they were in," says Ken Derr. "But they probably spent full time for a couple of months on the merger teams. Many must have spent 'the other full time' keeping up with the regular job. What happened, I'm sure, is that most people delegated a lot of responsibility during that time. That's not all bad either."

Richard Alberding, executive vice-president of marketing and international operations at Hewlett-Packard Company (HP), calls part-time adhocracy the tin-cup approach. Team leaders end up spending almost all their time fretting about support—"How do we get another $50,000 and two more heads?" and "God, is the boss going to cut our budget?"—instead of getting down to work. Alberding currently has a 20-person task force working on improving documentation

For the best results, companies should put core team members to work full time on the project.

26

for HP's various computer products. "I don't think the number of team members is as important as the fact that they are full-timers," he says. "They are the glue that helps us really accomplish something."

Part-time efforts can be effective, however, at some companies. Levi's Tom Tusher says that people on task forces at his company always have part-time duty. Trammell Crow is making major strides with four teams, all of them made up of part-timers. Phillip Williams at Times Mirror says, "We use lots of task forces, but the assignment is always TDY [temporary duty]."

Apple Computer Inc. executives in 1988 created an interesting hybrid adhocracy called the New Enterprise. Its purpose was no less grand than to look at the 21st-century business environment to see what sort of issues and opportunities might lurk in the company's future. The people who populated the team mainly describe themselves as "very part-time" (one estimated "four hours a week, maximum"). However, Apple's New Enterprise project manager, Sherie Berger, and director of strategic development, Nancy Farr, were pretty much full-time (they describe it as "double time") for the duration of the yearlong project.

Berger and Farr argue that if there had not been a cadre, albeit small, of full-time, midlevel team members, there would have been no way to make the project work. The project started with three full-timers—two consultants and Berger. Then for a period of a few months the core team grew to 12 full-time line people and several administrative folks. "It was very intense," says Berger. "Those people were not working 40-hour weeks; they were working whatever it took."

As the project progressed, most of Apple's senior people, including chief executive John Sculley, were involved at least part time. According to Randy Livingston, Apple's manager of corporate development, "The top three tiers of management were really engaged in the issues. We couldn't have done that if the team requirement had been full-time."

In sum, a typical task force might be composed of an executive godfather (often the chief executive, who spends

10:07 AM, Kansas City, Missouri. Message relayed.

With advanced satellite communications, our COSMOS® tracking network
can give you the status of your package anywhere
in the world. In just seconds.

one to two days a month working with the team and listening carefully to progress reports); a steering committee appointed by the godfather, which requires other executives to pay attention to the project at least once a quarter; a team leader, who spends anywhere from a third of his time to full time on the project; a small core of team members (two to seven), which devotes its full attention to the effort; and a fairly large contingent of part-timers who are in some way formally attached to the team and are expected to give it a few hours a week.

Most well-managed project teams are a variation on this theme. The size of the team, level of the sponsoring executive, nature of the steering committee, number of part-timers attached, duration of the various assignments, and other team arrangements all depend, like the idea of adhocracy itself, on the nature, magnitude, and importance of the issue or opportunity being addressed. The team structure will probably vary over time, as it did at Apple. It may start with only a few people, grow to a massive effort of virtual full-timers, and later transform itself into hundreds of people contributing part-time efforts.

HOSHIN

If full-time effort by some of the best and brightest people is often required, and executive involvement is crucial, then no one executive can have more than a few project-team efforts going at once. Managers I talk to these days admit to feeling overwhelmed by the issues of the day: global competition, deregulation, a fluctuating dollar. How, at the same time, to champion and embody such ineffable notions as total quality, just-in-time, excellence, renewal, innovation, time-based competition, entrepreneurship, intrapreneurship, employee involvement? How do you keep track of it all, make sense of it, let alone put it into effect?

My answer is simple. You can't. You must find a way to focus. Pick a few major issues or opportunities. The way these issues arise and gain support should not be too formalized. Companies miss too much by overplanning. What ought to be made rigorous for any executive, however, is the idea of always focusing on a few issues. Get teams going on those. Every executive ought to have at least one project team at work. More than a few teams, say three or four, will tax time and other necessary resources.

Which issues? Which opportunities? Richard Alberding describes a process that Hewlett-Packard recently adopted for selecting a few realistic issues on which to concentrate. "What you have to do is decide on two or three things you want to accomplish, not 50 or 100," he says. "About a year ago, we adopted a process called *hoshin*. In Japanese, that means 'direction.'"

At Hewlett-Packard each executive has several *hoshin*. The decision to adopt TQC (total quality control) at the company was once CEO John Young's *hoshin*. Young meant to improve quality in everything the company did by an order of magnitude, a factor of 10. Today, Young's *hoshin* is his widely publicized "time to break-even" program. He believes that HP can cut in half the time from product concept to profitable production.

Companies that fail at managing adhocracy usually lack the ability to concentrate resources on a few objectives. *Hoshin* is a relatively recent process at HP, and it doesn't always work. Executive vice-president of business development John Doyle sees the problem as a lack of will to make tough decisions. "Managers try to pile change on top of already fully occupied people," he says. "Then we don't put the organizational or financial resources behind the solution." The interesting question is, why not?

Doyle's answer takes us full circle. He believes that the commitment to do something wasn't there when the task force was created. Nobody asked "What if?" "What if the outcome requires more resources?" "What if the result suggests we abolish some treasured institution? Are we prepared to do it?"

In a fine summary of the problem of finding focus and keeping it—and in my mind a commentary on the American management scene in general—Doyle observes with a wry smile, "There's a lot more managerial won't than there is managerial will."

SUGGESTIONS
FOR GETTING STARTED

Adhocracy—and therefore a company's ability to take change in stride—will not work unless it is properly set up. Though every situation is different, I offer some general suggestions for getting the right start.

For Executives

Your main job is to create the process for effective problem-solving, not to solve the problem yourself. Therefore, your role at this stage is crucial.

■ If you are the chief executive, you should probably never lead project teams. The same applies if you report directly to the chief executive.

■ Make yourself available to your team on the first day of the project. Block time for regular interaction, which, depending on the importance of the effort, might mean getting together daily, weekly, or monthly—certainly no less frequently than once every quarter. Your role is to pay attention and act as coach, to help the team cut across traditional organizational boundaries, to encourage it to think boldly, and to ensure that it has the necessary resources.

■ Match the scope of the task force activity to the breadth of your own responsibilities. If solving the problem correctly requires companywide involvement, then the chief executive has to be involved and supportive. The project team should be responsible to an executive who has the power to make it happen.

■ Be fussy in picking task force leaders and in helping them select task force members. Reach down in the organization to find promising people.

■ Provide the financial resources necessary to make adhocracy work. In the rush to downsize and de-layer, most companies don't have the human resources to make adhocracy work as well as it should. If you agree that rapid change is here to stay and that team efforts work only when staffed with good people, then it's hard not to conclude that there is such a thing as being too lean and too mean.

■ Learn how to contribute to or effectively manage project teams. Create a special training program that teaches the techniques of group problem-solving, conflict resolution, listening skills, effective confrontation, coaching, and the like.

■ Don't start projects until you are committed to their importance. The two horns of today's organizational dilemma are the need to change and to decide where to allocate scarce resources. Focus is pivotal to adhocracy. Pick a few projects that are going nowhere and shut them down, and dedicate resources to the most promising ones.

For Team Leaders

Take on a project only when you hear clear noises from top managers, at the outset, that they will get involved and stay involved.

■ Concoct ways to keep top management's attention. From the start, plan regular reporting sessions to the sponsoring executive and the steering committee. If executive involvement is waning, recommend that the project be cut short or redirected.

■ Don't fret excessively about leading peers. Your job is to make sure the process works. You are not supposed to have the answer. Even if you think you do, it's best kept to yourself for a while.

■ Use the team-leader experience as a way of building your own leadership skills. Give enough direction to ensure that the team is getting results and meeting schedules, but spend most of your time listening to and encouraging others.

■ Negotiate with management for the best people you can find, and make sure that the makeup of the team covers the breadth of the problem. Ask for and use the power to replace a team member who isn't up to muster.

■ Obtain from upper management a clear understanding about the resources available to the team. If you don't think they're adequate, tell top management right away.

■ Commit only to budgets, schedules, and goals that you feel are realistic. The perception of your success will depend on management's expectations.

For Team Members

You will not have much influence in getting projects off to the right start, but you can do a few things to help ensure later success.

■ Do your best from the outset to understand the issue from top management's point of view. If you don't have the information or exposure to do that, ask for it.

■ Look at the assignment as a unique learning opportunity. You'll get exposed to points of view, parts of the organization, people, and skills that you would see in no other way.

■ Make sure that everyone in the process recognizes your full- or part-time commitment to the team. After establishing the proper replacement and support at your usual job, make a clean break. Don't clandestinely use the old job as an excuse to put off project work.

■ Talk back to the boss. Don't be nice and agree to serve on teams that you feel are destined to fail. If you're being asked to do the impossible, say so.

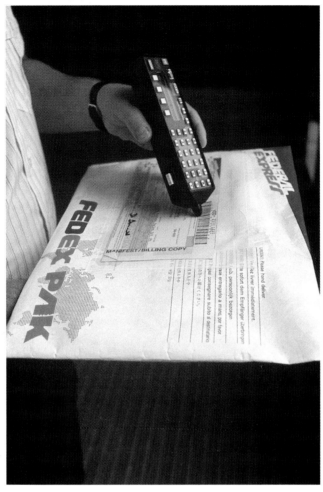

4:42 PM, London, England. The Supertracker encodes package information.

The Federal Express Supertracker® works with our computerized COSMOS tracking system to pinpoint the location of your package—from pick-up to delivery or anywhere in between.

An issue or opportunity is chosen, the team is formed, the starting conditions are right. Now what? Whether the team hits the ground running or limping depends on what happens during the first day or two.

THE KICKOFF: MAKE IT SPECIAL

CHAPTER

3

Dallas-based Trammell Crow Company ranks among the nation's largest commercial real estate developers. Along with Apple Computer, Hewlett-Packard, and Levi Strauss, Trammell Crow has been named one of the 100 best companies to work for in America. After a period of strong growth in the early 1980s, the company was beset by radical changes in its environment: industry overcapacity, tax laws that no longer sheltered real estate, depression in the oil states, and tougher loan requirements from banks and insurance companies—the main sources for real estate finance.

On February 16, 1989, after several months of planning, managing partner Joel Peterson launched four project teams to address some of these issues. Twenty company partners gathered for two days in Scottsdale, Arizona. Each of the partners would sponsor, lead, work on, or support teams. The meeting was carefully orchestrated to create a sense of urgency

Joel Peterson of Trammell Crow took his task forces away from the office to lend a sense of excitement to the company's project.

and excitement. Trammell Crow, the company's founder, was there to lend a hand and, symbolically, to convey the importance of the effort.

In his opening remarks, Peterson outlined the major issues, how they fit his vision for the company, and his determination to involve partners throughout the company as the project progressed. The partners were encouraged to ask questions— how the teams would work, what was expected, and so on. Then the teams adjourned to separate meeting rooms to figure out logistics and to talk in depth about the problems they'd been assigned.

Each team approached the day differently, but most began by listing tasks, breaking them into component parts, making initial work assignments, and scheduling follow-up meetings. One group got out its calendars and scheduled regular meetings right through to the end of the year. At the end of the day the teams reconvened to report their progress. The meeting concluded with a statement of each team's commitment to the work it planned to accomplish and a schedule.

Peterson's zeal, the setting in Arizona, Crow's visible support, the importance of the issues, and the uniqueness of the event all helped create the sense that something special was going on. Peterson underscored that feeling by stating repeatedly that every facet of company policy was fair game. "In this real estate market, there are no experts," he said. "The future is uncertain. We're going to work on the gut issues of running this business *together*."

I strongly believe that every ad hoc endeavor deserves a distinctive kickoff. The meeting's length, setting, and tone must fit the occasion and company culture, but even small projects should begin with a meeting of the whole team. The sponsoring executive should give the first speech, wave the flag throughout, and render suitable closing remarks.

Raychem Corporation kicked itself into adhocracy and a whole new strategic orbit with the most dramatic new program launch I know of. Another company on the list of the 100 best to work for, Raychem makes materials with memories—for example, plastic tubing that shrinks when heated and is used to insulate the electric cabling in aircraft. In 1957, chairman and chief executive Paul Cook started the company with $50,000 in the proverbial garage. It measured 4,000 square feet. "Today," jokes president and chief operating officer Bob Halperin, "we have two garages." They total some five million square feet, employ 11,000 people, and generate annual sales of more than one billion dollars.

Every year until 1981 Raychem had strategic-review sessions. "We had the kind that good business practice says you're supposed to have," Halperin says. "We managed to stay awake through most of them because we felt it was our duty." Finally, he and Cook decided that the sessions were moving them nowhere. They felt they needed to find a way to galvanize management, to drive home the point that things were going to change dramatically. They settled on an annual planning retreat at Pajaro Dunes, California.

For managers used to clarity and action, getting a task force up and running may be the most frustrating part of any project.

The meeting began in the usual soporific way. Suddenly it was interrupted by a horrendous racket. A fleet of helicopters, bearing signs that read IMAGINATION, INNOVATION, RISK-TAKING, landed right outside the conference room. The pilots, dressed as prison guards, strode into the meeting room and herded the group members into the waiting helicopters, then flew them about 50 miles south to Big Sur. There they were met, oceanside, by a small elephant wearing a sign forecasting Raychem's growth goals through the 1980s. The elephant was followed by a string of camels. More messages: IMAGINATION, TECHNICAL PIONEERS. Last in line was a huge elephant announcing the company's target growth rate for the early 1990s. By the end of the retreat, one big message was clear: Business as usual was out at Raychem.

Though the company will not meet the growth goals it set for itself in the early 1980s, Halperin says, "We wouldn't have changed anything about that meeting. We've dramatically broadened our technology base, secured position in entirely new and large markets, and we are close to making Japan our number-one offshore market. We're a different company."

For managers used to clarity and action, getting a task force up and running may be the most frustrating part of any project. At the Trammell Crow meeting in Scottsdale, the mood was tentative, a mixture of enthusiasm and anxiety. Trammell Crow's uncertain future was on everyone's mind, and it felt good to address those problems head-on. But could the project teams really resolve issues this big and this complex? "Our people were used to doing real estate deals and had never seen a process like this before," Peterson says. "There wasn't much confidence that it would work."

Structure helps to allay such fears and frustrations. Remember football coach Bill Walsh's well-rehearsed opening plays. Imagine how it would feel to be thrown together suddenly with people you don't know well, with no game plan and little understanding of what lies ahead. At one of the worst kickoff meetings I can remember, the first day was spent brainstorming strategy and discussing "what's wrong with the business." The issues were unfocused, and the meetings were unstructured. A well-meant effort backfired as the participants dwelt on the negative and ended up convinced that things were much worse than they had thought. Certainly they had no hope for improvement.

Structure counts in another sense. Researchers have found that a common glitch in group efforts is the tendency to pounce on solutions. Groups jump straight to answers even before they have defined the problem, collected information, or considered alternatives. As organizational theorist Karl Weick pointed out, "Activities that are not directly related to producing solutions [planning, discussion, generating alternatives, withholding evaluation] are not likely to occur unless substantial efforts are made to override the group's solution-mindedness."

Trammell Crow's Joel Peterson has come up with a nifty way to satisfy the group need for answers without closing off alternatives. "Fantasize the ideal end product," he suggests. "Write it down. Imagine that the effort has run its course and that it has been a smash success. What would we have accomplished that will make Trammell Crow a better place?" By asking those questions, he was able to strike a nice balance between focus and flexibility. And he kept the mood upbeat.

Chevron routinely starts projects with a simple sheet of paper that outlines the team's purpose, objectives, start date, team composition, anticipated result, and hoped-for sunset date. Vice-chairman Jim Sullivan showed me several examples and seemed a little embarrassed that one of them took all of three pages. Sullivan still remembers his first encounter with the one-pager, when he was asked to serve on his very first task force as a new, young employee: "They put that in front of you so you could clearly see what they were about. Nothing was hidden. Without threat or hidden agenda, you felt pretty good about it."

Special meetings are crucial as the ad hoc effort gets up and running. But how do you turn quick acceleration into lasting momentum? Peterson called the managing partners of Trammell Crow together for a second meeting at the end of February 1989, this time in Houston. The team leaders asked plenty of tough questions. Peterson responded with more details and a strategic framework, and the partners agreed to meet every other month. The struggle for focus was under way.

9:23 PM, Bruges, Belgium. Crosstown delivery.

Sending a package overseas? Federal Express has over
28,000 couriers worldwide who can deliver. On time.

"The overwhelming plus is that [the partners] own the problems now," Peterson says. "They regard them as a legitimate part of their responsibility. They've turned out some very thoughtful and imaginative work." Team members have developed strong bonds, and Trammell Crow people now seem confident that they can beat the issues that once had them hog-tied.

STRUCTURING THE UNKNOWN

What teams should do between meetings is fairly straightforward—and very difficult. You feel as though you're lost at sea on the legendary dark and stormy night. You have a good idea of where you want to go and of your general position, but you have no idea what lies ahead, and your charts are lousy. How do you continue to make progress through these unfamiliar seas?

Think of the process as a scientific investigation. Frame several hypotheses, get the facts, reframe the hypotheses, get more facts, and so on, until the answers to the major issues emerge. In my experience, few project teams would win gold stars for their discipline in following this approach.

Here's an example of this process in successful action. A large mining company in Australia was trying to set a new strategic direction. Specifically, the issue became, how do we spend excess cash flow generated by increased demand from the Japanese for coking coal? The initial hypothesis: Buy more coal reserves. Facts were gathered to answer the following questions raised by that hypothesis: Would high Japanese demand continue? How available was high-grade coal in Australia? Which companies with coal reserves in Australia or elsewhere in the world might begin to compete for Japan's business?

After a few months' work, the team concluded that Japanese demand had always been cyclical and would probably remain so. Relative to worldwide competition, this company's coal was expensive. In the likely event of a flattening or downturn in Japanese demand for metallurgical coal, the company would slip back into marginal profitability—i.e., business as usual. High Japanese demand was only a temporary aberration that had improved profits and cash flow.

New hypothesis: Find ways to make the existing mines more efficient, and spend excess cash flow on that. More fact-gathering revealed that there were only two sources of inefficiency: an unusually high incidence of union trouble—strikes, slowdowns, work stoppages—and incessant trouble in keeping the continuous miners (the machines that cut coal away from the coal face) up and operating. The facts showed that on a typical day the continuous miners were up and operating only 15 percent of the time. The team started calling them discontinuous miners.

Next hypothesis: Find better ways to deal with the miners' union and improve continuous-miner technologies. New facts: Most of the strike activity was related to recurring safety problems, especially in and around the continuous-mining operation. Final hypothesis: Efficiency and labor relations can be improved only through changes in working conditions and technology. In fact, just getting the discontinuous miners to operate 20 percent of the time would increase the net present value of a single mine by roughly $100 million.

I've simplified the story considerably, of course. This sort of work is messier, less structured, and less clear than I've made it sound. But the underlying discipline was always there. Hypothesis. Fact-gathering. New hypothesis.

Effective management of adhocracy is just as important for small companies as for large ones—perhaps more so because so much of life in small companies is ad hoc. Molecular Devices Corporation is a 100-person start-up in the biotechnology business. "There were two scientists when I joined the company," says chief executive Gary Steele. "The company was, in a sense, only a project. Now we have launched multiple products—seven in the last 28 months. We're now shipping in 19 countries."

Steele is an expert on project management. For years, he and I worked together at McKinsey & Company. He left to become a senior executive at Genentech Inc., where his primary responsibility was nudging, beseeching, galvanizing, and coaching people from diverse scientific disciplines to work as a team to get products developed, approved by the Food and Drug Administration, and into the market.

Every product at Molecular Devices is launched by a project team. Steele uses a launching process similar to the one described in the mining-company example. What I call hypotheses, he calls assumptions. "To get everybody on the same page," Steele says, "the team begins by writing out fairly detailed assumptions: 'Here's the product we're defining; here's the way we're staffing it; here are the goals (timing to launch, movement into manufacturing, transition into alpha and beta sites); and here's the technical approach.'

"Assumptions are a way to help bridge a set of different languages. The electrical engineer and the chemist working together really need a common language because their worlds are very different."

Assumptions not only set general direction but also established such critical details for Molecular Devices as the size of a bottle. "If the assumptions change on you, then we need to know it," Steele tells his teams. "We may need to change direction or even kill the project," he says. "If you're not clear on the assumptions, what happens is that you head off in wrong directions with inertia that you just can't stop."

Steele offers an example: "We might find we've invested $3 million only to learn that a rubber stopper in the top of the bottle of one of our reagents is incompatible with one of the ingredients. Holding to the idea that the rubber stopper would work could have killed us."

In an imperfect world, you can't ever know precisely where any given path will lead. Write out what you expect. Test it. If you're right, inch forward; if not, change direction and repeat the process. At what intervals should you stop and reassess your assumptions? "We revisit assumptions quarterly because the company meets quarterly," Steele says. "But I remember a project launch where the team met every morning at 8 a.m. to review the assumptions and question every detail."

Steele's assumptions wouldn't mean much without some sort of mechanism for immediately redirecting activity when new information invalidates an assumption. At Molecular Devices, Steele uses a metaphorical system of red and yellow

Gary Steele of Molecular Devices recommends writing out assumptions to create a common language among people from various divisions.

flags. Employees learn about it at their first orientation meeting. It's that important.

"A yellow flag means 'I don't even know if I'm right. I haven't investigated it thoroughly; it's just a hunch. But I'm raising my hand because I think there's a problem. Our assumption may be wrong.' The red flag says, 'I'm pulling the cord on the train. I'm stopping the wheels at the risk of people falling over. There is a problem here, folks. I'm sure an important assumption is wrong, and I think it's so serious that I exercise my right to pull the cord.'"

Steele's system of assumptions and colored flags probably seems chaotic. But I doubt that there is any other way to make progress through unknown territory. As Steele says, "It'll save you a ton of money if this system is part of everyone's mind-set."

INFORMATION: THE FACTS OF LIFE

The early phases of project work are mostly spent gathering, analyzing, and testing facts. Typically, teams are stymied by their own lack of imagination in each of these activities. An eclectic outlook helps.

Teams usually begin fact-finding with an intense interview phase. Chevron's vice-president of human resources, Lou Fernandez, is putting the finishing touches on what he calls the performance-management program (PMP), designed to improve employees' abilities to manage their own work and others'. PMP is the work of two task forces, one that studied performance-measurement systems, the other compensation. Altogether the teams conducted some 1,200 interviews with Chevron people.

Typically the bulk of interviewing is internal. Less common, but perhaps more effective, is extensive external interviewing. Who has already solved a similar problem? What do our customers or suppliers—or even competitors—have to say? What can we learn from them? In fact, Chevron's performance-management teams started their work that way. Both teams began by identifying and interviewing executives at companies that seemed to have excellent appraisal and compensation systems.

At Trammell Crow, a team exploring compensation alternatives started its work by talking with executives outside the company who hire talented people and manage in a partnership style: lawyers, investment bankers, other respected real estate developers, accountants, consultants, and headhunters. A team looking at capital policy interviewed investment bankers and other financial players who offered information and opinion on future sources for real estate capital. The resulting data became a major fulcrum for rethinking at Trammell Crow.

A team at Intel Corporation used this approach to set up a new disability plan. Plan administrator Maureen Shiells says that a number of other companies' approaches were analyzed. One finding: "The people at Gallo wine seemed to be doing an excellent job with half the staff that we might use. We've learned a lot from Gallo about simplifying our own system."

Approaches to getting information ought to be limited only by the team's imagination. In Australia, an exploration team member decided to read through old explorers' journals. "A description of some cliffs in far northern Queensland had the feel of bauxite about it," he recalls. Intrigued, he convinced the team to investigate. His careful reading resulted in a major bauxite discovery.

The most neglected information-collection technique is the experiment. Bureaucracies abhor experiments because they mean mistakes, and people get penalized for mistakes. But in uncharted terrain, especially new-product-development work, how else do you learn? Market research doesn't work—no one has any relevant experience with the new gizmo. The only thing you can do is dip a toe into the water.

Children's Television Workshop, the company that started *Sesame Street*, needed a good way to find out what its 3- and 4-year-old audience really thought of the programs. Team members took newly developed segments to day-care centers and showed them to the children, while also projecting very distracting slides on a screen near the monitor. If the kids paid more attention to the slides than to the show, the team knew there was a problem with the segment. The company still tries out new material this way.

Any management decision involves both fact and value content. Most teams don't distinguish between the two. Everything is treated as a value judgment. Arguing is easier, and often more fun, than getting the facts.

Just as value judgments aren't the same as information, so is information different from data. We live in a society that is data-rich and information-poor. We're so inundated with numbers and breaking news that few of us can figure out what's really going on. Information and understanding come from forced comparisons. A large part of the consultant's magic is in graphic presentations that compare one set of facts with another. An example of this comes from Richard Saul Wurman's book *Information Anxiety*: "To say that an acre equals 6,272,640 square inches is factual and accurate," he writes. "However, to say that an acre is about the size of an American football field without the end zones is not as accurate, but it's much more understandable." Data are not information; translating fact to understanding means relating data to something you already know and can visualize.

To make comparisons easier, keep in mind the importance of a written assumption or hypothesis. Think of it as the stake in the ground that marks your progress.

> **A**ny management decision involves both fact and value content. Most teams don't distinguish between the two.

DECLARE WAR ON THE PROBLEM

Whenever possible, the trappings of adhocracy should reflect its urgency. Few managers realize the power they have to make change happen simply by showing the whole organization that they take a project seriously. One way they can convey this sense of importance is by setting up a "war room" for teams. This is a room, or complex of rooms, set aside especially for the project. People report there each day, rather than to their own offices. Desks and telephones are set up for team members, and research and secretarial support are stationed close at hand. All the team's documents, workstations, computers, and files are located there as well. Typically, the walls are papered with ideas from brainstorming sessions, work schedules, mission statements, and cartoons that poke fun at the effort and the team members.

7:27 PM, Minneapolis, Minnesota. Package dropped off.

With thousands of convenient Drive-Thru Centers, Drop Boxes, and Service Centers, Federal Express has the most extensive worldwide network in the air express industry.

The symbolism of the war room may be its most important feature. It says to the team members, "This is your prime job for the moment." It says to the whole organization, "This work has top priority; we're giving it special space." My colleague and veteran project manager George Glaser notes, "I think the war room is an excellent device, largely because there is a certain amount of show biz connected with it—the graphics, the fact that the walls are covered, the fact that the room is used for no other purpose. It raises everyone's level of consciousness."

The other clear function of the war room is that it forces communication among team members. One of the funny and sad examples I saw of unsuccessful adhocracy was a team that was supposed to put together a new information system for a Fortune 500 company. The team was formed with good people, full-time, from both the food and data processing sides of the house. It never got anywhere.

Later I made a case study of the team's behavior over time. The people involved never met as a full team. The data processing guys and the food folks weren't thrown together in the same room, although they easily could have been. When they traveled to field locations, often at the same time, they stayed in separate hotels. The systems people liked upscale hotels where they could exercise. The food people, feeling budget pressure, stayed in cheaper motels. The opportunities to meet and work together were many and easy. But the two halves of the team behaved throughout like oil and water.

War rooms aren't always possible. At Trammell Crow, key team members were spread across the country and so were unable to give full-time effort to the projects. But much else can be done to lend symbolic support. Trammell Crow is run by a management board—Joel Peterson and the top partners in the company. The four project teams were pulled primarily from the board, a signal to everyone in the company of hands-on support from top management. And because many board members were team members, Peterson says, "the process and the work of the teams became the board's agenda; it got that kind of dignity."

Settings away from the office can also help convey a sense of importance to the team's efforts. Among my favorite settings were those we used for progress review and training during a McKinsey & Company project that led to *In Search of Excellence*. The settings were a dude ranch in Wyoming, a big estate near Dartmoor, in England, and a chateau in Evian, France.

The pattern we followed at the dude ranch typified the meetings. Hard work in the morning. Lunch and a long break for fishing, horseback riding, and hiking until five in the afternoon. More hard work until about seven. Dinner, drinks, and some uninhibited business and social conversation in the evening. Few telephones. There were plenty of planned diversions, but the remote location made it impossible to get away from the issues at hand. Both the schedule and the setting symbolized the whole point of our project: we were moving in a new and different direction.

Mundane as it sounds, the simple process of getting regular meetings on everyone's calendars also symbolizes the importance of project work. Think about it. What is the real, scarce resource in any organization? The time of its best people. Small shifts in the calendars of those folks signal big changes in an organization's focus.

In some cases, daily meetings are useful, especially where a war room is feasible and the project is large, crucial, and on a tight schedule—a new product launch, for instance. Consultant George Glaser has run dozens of projects this way. "[Daily meetings] create an entirely different atmosphere than that of the team that has only monthly meetings," he says. "People go off to the winds for the next 30 days. Then they all come back and have excuses as long as your arm about what didn't happen: Sally was sick, Mary Jo's dog got hit by a truck, there was a fire in the wastebasket—more excuses than you can imagine, all of which means not much progress was made during the past month."

Face-to-face meetings are clearly best. As a substitute, regularly scheduled telephone conference calls can help team members trade ideas and stay on track. Any of us who have participated in these conferences, though, know how uncongenial they can be for creative interchange. Technology may help. Videoconferencing and electronic mail have recently become commonplace at many companies, such as Apple Computer, as the best substitutes for face-to-face meetings. I talked with educator Warren Bennis about adhocracy, a concept he's been writing about for 21 years. "If I were to redo *The Temporary Society*," he says, "I would certainly have some sort of a chart showing the interrelationship between technology and asynchrony [his term for the inability to get together]."

LOCAL HEROES

The old saw that says "The difficult we do immediately; the impossible takes a little longer" characterizes effective adhocracy. The best teams seem to be driven by big ideas and targets that seem impossible. Big targets create a sense of adventure that attracts the best people in the organization. "Impossible" goals force people to forget old we-they boundaries and pull together. The purpose, not the box on the chart, becomes the organizing principle. Big ideas force rethinking of old systems. Instead of saying, "Let's take this old machine and put the pedal to the metal," the team says, "Let's redesign the whole machine."

That's the kind of challenge that now has the folks at Trammell Crow turned on. The totality of the effort is no less than a rethinking of the way they go about their business in the new real estate environment. Everything is under scrutiny, from the way they raise money and approach the market to the way they reward themselves. Peterson keeps admonishing the teams: "There are no sacred cows." In most companies, this kind of thinking takes place only behind closed doors, in the executive suite. But at Trammell Crow all the partners get to participate in plotting the future. The challenge, coupled with Peterson's obvious faith in the partners' ability, has filled them with pride and a feeling that, indeed, this company is special.

Part of the magic at Hewlett-Packard is chief executive John Young's habit of regularly announcing some grand "impossible" objective. Young's latest charge to the company: cut product break-even time in half. If it used to take four years from conception to break-even, do it now in two. Early results have validated this target. Computer printers, which used to take 54 months to develop, can now be put into profitable production in 22 months.

General Electric Company did the same thing with its sleepy circuit-breaker business. Faced with tough competition from the likes of Siemens and Westinghouse, GE concluded that it had to change the way it produced circuit breakers or get out of that business. The company put together a team of manufacturing, design, and marketing experts. Their mission was to overhaul the manufacturing process and cut the time between order and delivery from three weeks to three days.

A nonprofit homebuilder, Bridge Housing Corporation, may be the quintessential example of adhocracy propelled by big ideas. Bridge ranks 125th on the list of the biggest builders in the United States. The company builds attractive, high-quality, below-market-price housing in places like San Francisco, where the median house costs more than $250,000.

Bridge's top officers, president Don Terner and executive vice-president Carol Galante, explain how the process works. A group of people, drawn from the Bridge bureaucracy, puts together deal structures that are predicated on heroic political concessions and financial arrangements. "We can produce where the private sector can't," says Terner, "if we can match them on normal operating effectiveness and beat them in bringing our heroic assumptions to life."

The Pacific Oaks area, just south of San Francisco, had frustrated three private companies because of development restrictions. "We assumed that by flying our banner of public purpose and excellence in design we could go to the voters for a special election and get them to exempt this property from restrictions on housing density," says Terner. "We mounted a campaign to go to the voters, and we won with 82 percent of the vote. We won even in the precinct where the project was located, which almost never happens.

"We mounted a grass-roots campaign. Seniors in the community got involved and had more fun than at a bake sale. They hung posters. And with their help we turned a lemon into lemonade. What's more, everybody was a winner. American Savings, the S&L that had the piece of

Don Terner, president of Bridge Housing Corporation, structures his projects around heroic assumptions that force rethinking of old ideas.

dog property, won because it got book value for the property. The people felt like winners because they were doing something that was perceived as positive by an overwhelming majority. We felt like winners because we built 140 units where others had struck out. Best of all, the consumers were winners. They got $390-a-month rents."

Don Terner captures the power, drama, adventure, and excitement that comes when adhocracy is at its finest.

SUGGESTIONS FOR STAYING ON TRACK

The notion that adhocracy should be managed just as carefully as bureaucracy is new. Because of that, managers commonly throw a task force together, get no results, and have no idea why it didn't work. Following are a few rules of thumb to prevent that from happening.

For Executives

■ Set the tone on day one. Get the whole team together in a special place. Attend opening and closing meetings and special events. Drop in on team meetings, wander about, but keep your distance. Arrange for some play as well as work.

■ Insist that the team's approach be rigorous. Train your people in hypothesis-development and fact-gathering.

■ Use symbols and settings to continue reminding the team of its importance. The simplest symbolic tool is blocking time on your calendar. Other symbolic tools include war rooms, regular reporting sessions, and special locations for meetings.

■ Make the work exciting; put a little adventure into it. I do this by managing expectations: I commit to the client only what I know the team can achieve, but I also challenge the team to go beyond anything it has ever done before.

For Team Leaders and Members

■ Get used to working with hypotheses or assumptions. Each team member should have the power to raise flags. Insist that progress reviews follow a format that says, "Here's what we assumed; here's what we've learned; here are the new assumptions."

■ Project work can be frightening or it can be exhilarating. You can make the difference by clarifying assumptions, gathering facts, experimenting to test those assumptions, and waving the flag if something is awry.

■ Encourage imaginative approaches to getting the facts. Give special attention to the role of experimentation. Make sure team members know that making some mistakes is okay.

■ Be both rigorous and creative. Rigor comes from being explicit about assumptions and waving flags. Creativity comes from resourceful approaches to getting data and from making imaginative comparisons.

10:07 AM, Hong Kong. Morning flight arrives on time.

When you send your package Federal Express—
domestic or international—we take care of your shipment
every step of the way.

GETTING RESULTS

We Americans are pretty good at looking ahead, anticipating future events, and laying plans to cope with them. We're awful at implementation. We envision the outcome of our work as recommendations, not results. The goal of well-run ad-hocracy is not a good report. It's change.

HANDOFFS STRICTLY PROHIBITED

We're used to thinking sequentially: get the facts, analyze them, make decisions, and then implement. We consider implementation to be the last step in the process, something to be done by someone else. Hewlett-Packard's executive vice-president of business development, John Doyle, says that even his consistently innovative company has been dogged by this problem.

"We have lots of ways of putting together task forces from disparate parts of the organization. I think we do that quite well," he says. "I also think we run them quite well. We have a wonderfully cooperative organization of intelligent and motivated people who do first-class work on analysis and synthesis. The findings are always first class. But when we have problems, they almost always lie in implementation."

Doyle describes a recent team effort: "It was the very best task force that I've been involved in. We came out with an excellent report a year ago. Our recommendations weren't just clear; they were crucial." A year and a half has gone by since the team made its report. "Nothing was done," says Doyle.

Looking back, he has no doubt about what doomed the project. After the recommendations were made, implementation was handed off to someone else. "That was the wrong

John Doyle of Hewlett-Packard: "We have lots of ways of putting together task forces. . . . But when we have problems, they almost always lie in implementation."

decision. The team doing the work had been learning for 18 months," he says. "They had this vast reservoir of information that would have made implementation relatively easy. There had been enough analysis that synthesis was possible. There was enough exposure that intuition was viable."

Doyle says he was too overburdened at the time to question the decision to hand off implementation. "But the people who took it over had none of the understanding that the team had built up during the course of the work," he says. "They were not invested in it. It was just another task. Plunk. This is no criticism of the new people at all; they are very able."

I immediately empathized with Doyle's lament. I've seen this happen again and again. First-rate people. Excellent analysis. Solid recommendations. Token implementation.

Chevron's salty chief financial officer, Lee McGraw, says the same pattern explains why big consulting teams haven't worked for his company: "Even if they submit a great report, they don't have their skin on it." He has recently assigned the task of consolidating credit-card centers for Chevron to an in-house team because, he says, "the guy leading the effort is the guy who's got to make the SOB work when it's done."

The problem is not consultants, per se. Chevron uses consultants regularly and successfully to support teams. The problem is the handoff. The people doing the work can't transfer their understanding or their zest for making something happen to others who haven't been involved. What's more, people are simply more responsive and practical when they know they are the ones who have to live with whatever they've recommended.

IT'S MY BABY

Looking back on my consulting career, I find that a single factor distinguishes a great result from a good study. That factor is the massive involvement of clients in the project. Client team members, people serving as liaisons on steering committees and assigned temporarily, outnumbered the consultants by at least 5 to 1—sometimes by as much as 20 to 1.

"People love their own children," explains Stanford University professor Harold J. Leavitt. "Other people's babies, well, they're okay." Similarly, people love their own ideas. They respond well to processes in which their ideas influence decisions.

At Ford, an adhocracy called Team Taurus is the most dramatic example I've seen of Leavitt's concept in action. Launched in the summer of 1980, Team Taurus eventually set the pattern for the way the company is organized today.

Lewis Veraldi, vice-president of engineering and manufacturing at Ford, was the ideal team leader. In 1970 he had been a design engineer at Ford. He asked for a three-year assignment in manufacturing, to find out for himself why design and manufacturing seemed to be constantly at war. Working double shifts, he soon had a very different perspective from his cohorts in design. Time after time Veraldi watched the manufacturing side sabotage the designers' "babies." And why not? Manufacturing had virtually no input into the design of the car, hence no personal stake in its success.

Lewis Veraldi, a vice-president at Ford, brought manufacturers and designers together to produce the company's highly successful Taurus.

In 1973 Veraldi was asked to head the $840 million Fiesta small-car project in West Germany, then the biggest program in Ford's 70-year history. Friction between manufacturing and design was so intense that design engineers weren't even allowed inside assembly plants. One of Veraldi's first moves was to bring manufacturing people into the design process, asking them, "How can we design this car to make your job easier?" It was the right question.

Despite the success of the Fiesta in Germany, Ford was awash in red ink by the early 1980s. Losses in both 1980 and 1981 were more than one billion dollars. The company desperately needed a winning entry in the midsize-car market, where volume and profit potential were highest. Management, led by chief executive Philip Caldwell, believed that warmed-over versions of current products wouldn't do. It took guts to fund the new $3.25 billion project that would result in the Taurus.

A bold challenge from top management created the heroic, exciting atmosphere that I discussed in the previous chapter. Donald Petersen, then Ford's president, pressed the Taurus group to "give us a car that would make you proud, one that you would like to drive." Caldwell played a relentless devil's advocate. "Why should I or anyone buy this car?" he kept asking the team.

Broad participation made the difference. The company had previously built cars sequentially, a process that Ford people called the over-the-wall syndrome. Designers would do their bit, then pass the work over the wall to engineering. Engineering would work on it, then toss it over the wall to manufacturing. Then over the wall to sales and marketing. At every stage in the process, people looked back over the walls, muttering, "Why the hell did they do it that way?" By the time the car went over the last few walls—assembly and then the showroom—it was too late to change anything.

On Team Taurus, design and production advanced in tandem. Assembly, marketing, and service people took part in the car's development from conception. Veraldi believed— and the Taurus's stunning success bore him out—that if everyone with a stake in the outcome was brought in early, quality would improve. He cast a wide net in seeking suggestions. "Four and a half years before job one [the first car off the production line], we visited assembly plants, manufacturing facilities, major suppliers, the Service Managers Council, and insurance companies," he says. "We asked them, 'If you were doing this kind of car, what would you like to see in it?'"

Planning director John Risk worked directly under Veraldi. "I'd be down at the Atlanta assembly plant. I'd climb in a car as it went down the assembly line and introduce myself. Then I'd ask for ideas," he says. "In one case, I saw two people juggling an instrument panel, so I asked them what might make that job easier. They suggested a small locator pin that would secure the panel in the same place every time." Risk estimates that asking questions on the assembly line alone yielded 1,000 ideas that the company used.

Projects organized like this—involving hundreds of people almost from day one—are hard to diagram and feel out of control but are incredibly effective. Why? First of all, they're more innovative. How else would Ford have come up with those 1,000 workable ideas?

Second, projects like Team Taurus cut product-cycle time

and cost. Though the Taurus has its roots in a project started in 1977, it had no real impetus until top management got behind it in 1980. Measured from that point, Ford estimates that the team approach cut development time for the Taurus by at least a year and saved $300 million in development costs.

This approach is counter to conventional project work, even today. Charging ahead on all fronts would seem likely to slow development time and increase costs because of potential confusion and duplication of activity. In reality the process is more efficient. It encourages communication and problem-solving at even the lowest levels. Conflicts get resolved before they become battles.

Third, projects that involve everyone ennoble the implementation process. Many executives and consultants think of implementation as something others do—others who are not quite as smart. I got a letter the other day from a consultant who referred to "the scut work of implementation." The letter reeked with disdain for the process.

Finally, projects organized like Taurus mesh perfectly with my vision of the requirements for successful implementation. The groundwork for implementation starts when the project is launched, not after the team has done its work. Thus the project becomes everyone's baby; everyone has a chance to contribute and raise objections. As the project nears completion, hundreds, or even thousands, of the people whose support is needed to make it succeed are already committed.

Stanford professor Harold J. Leavitt: "Implementation involves changing other people's behavior, and therefore it is a highly emotional activity."

"Implementation involves changing other people's behavior, and therefore it is a highly emotional activity," says Professor Leavitt. "Everything the social sciences know about changing behavior says that people change for emotional reasons far more than for rational reasons." Processes that appeal to our emotions are those that invite our input and take our suggestions seriously.

Four years after its introduction, the Ford Taurus and its Mercury equivalent, the Sable, are selling faster than ever. In 1988 Ford earned a stunning 25 percent on equity. And despite several new model introductions by General Motors in early 1989, Ford continues to build its market share in the midsize category.

11:35 PM, Memphis, Tennessee. Charter fleet assigned.

If your domestic or overseas freight shipments require customized service, Federal Express offers air charter service with our fleet of B-747s, DC-10s and B-727s.

2:11 AM, Memphis, Tennessee. Heavyweight shipment ready for take-off.

Our Heavyweight[sm] Service handles virtually any size package
to virtually any destination. In fact, the Federal Express system handles
up to 14 million pounds daily.

THE BEST OF BOTH WORLDS

No, we're not watching the death throes of bureaucracy. Tomorrow's excellent company will be both bureaucracy and adhocracy. Neither form will dominate. Though ad hoc work will no longer be thought of as something done off-line, bureaucracy will not disappear. We still need people in charge. We still need specialists within divisions.

Nobody understands this better than Bob Swanson, a founder and the chief executive of Genentech Inc., the successful West Coast biotechnology company. Swanson says that the project-team approach is the only way to navigate the tortuous process of product development in this esoteric field. Genentech spent six years getting one of its products, a human-growth hormone, from the idea stage through testing and Food and Drug Administration approval, and finally to market. When engrossed in such an intense and protracted project, people easily lose their professional edge. At Genentech, Swanson makes sure that molecular biologists, protein chemists, pharmacologists, and others have a home in the bureaucracy. They need to interact constantly with the top people in their own functional groups to stay current in their fields.

Moreover, a successful ad hoc effort can actually change the bureaucracy. The process can give executives a feeling of exhilaration, but it also arouses fear of the unknown. Unless those in the bureaucracy are kept in touch with what the project team is doing and why, they will find ways to make sure adhocracy fails. They're not being malicious, just human. Change is threatening. Adhocracy, therefore, must be organized to work in concert with bureaucracy.

Part of the genius of Team Taurus was its delicate maneuvering in and out of the bureaucracy. The organizational chart for the team was drawn as a huge pie with an inner and outer ring. The center ring, labeled "the car-program development group," included Lew Veraldi and the other heavy hitters: planning director John Risk, chief designer John Telnack, and chief engineer A. L. Guthrie. This was the core of the team, the flywheel that made the program go. Included in the outer ring were all the pieces of the bureaucracy that had to be integrated into the effort: design, component engineering, manufacturing, service, purchasing, legal, sales and marketing, and management review.

Within the outer ring, linked together and radiating out from the center like spokes on a bicycle wheel, were hexagons, circles, and boxes. A hexagon represented a person who was completely dedicated to the Taurus program. Circles stood for people and units that had a defined liaison role with the team. Boxes were review committees. Some of the people in the outer circle worked full time with the Team Taurus core group. Others stayed in their various functional roles but had no assignment other than to support Taurus. Still others had part-time or review responsibilities.

The relationship between adhocracy and bureaucracy was clear. This arrangement is in dramatic contrast to some I've seen in which the project team charges off to do its work, does not keep others in the organization informed, and builds such deep resentment that it can't get even the best recommendations implemented.

The Team Taurus approach was so successful that in 1986, shortly after the Taurus came out, Ford adopted the same approach on all new-product development. The company has had mixed results. Three products that Ford has introduced since then—a new model of the rakish Lincoln Continental, introduced in December 1987; the slope-nosed 1989 Thunderbird; and its sibling, the Mercury Cougar—are all successful. The Continental has been a sellout since its introduction, and outside automotive experts have praised the T-Bird. But the teamwork in creating these products was far from seamless: there wasn't the same easy fit between bureaucracy and adhocracy as in the Taurus project. The approach was introduced midway through the Continental and the T-Bird programs, and the people working on those teams just didn't feel that the project was their baby.

The importance of linking adhocracy and bureaucracy can't be overstated. At Chevron, chief executive Ken Derr knew the company needed the support of Gulf people to make the

The Team Taurus approach was so successful that Ford adopted it for all new-product development.

merger work. "The scope was so big and the time was so limited that we couldn't get bogged down in the normal approval process [the bureaucracy]," says Derr. "We also knew that we couldn't just send guys out there who would ignore the leaders of the various functions."

Several steps were taken at Chevron to keep bureaucracy and adhocracy working side by side. First, top management insisted that the deal be called a merger, not a takeover or an acquisition. Second, each of the 37 teams was co-chaired by one person from Chevron and one from Gulf, another move to win the support of the Gulf bureaucracy. The top functional executives in every area being reviewed by teams were designated sponsoring executives. Teams reported both to the ad hoc structure under Derr (and his counterpart from Gulf, Jim Murdy) and to the sponsoring executives. For example, the top exploration manager in each company would be designated sponsoring executive; the exploration task force would be run by co-chairmen who came from one or two levels down in exploration. Finally, minority reports were accepted. People who didn't agree with team conclusions had a way to express their dissent.

"READ THE BLOODY METER"

Because adhocracy can so easily run off track, it needs monitoring. In concept, monitoring is simple: set milestones, measure results, and follow up. But enacting the concept takes effort. "To make new forms of organization work, you need measures," says Hewlett-Packard's John Doyle. "You have to define what you plan to measure, you need a system that measures, and then you have to read the bloody meter."

What measurement system is appropriate for adhocracy? I think that you should first set forth the basic objective, as Ford did with the Taurus when it decided to build a car that was "best in class," i.e., the best in the world in its price and size category. Then you must arbitrarily break the project up into bite-sized chunks. The end of each chunk is a milestone.

Chunking, as I call it, took the form of a key-events schedule on the Taurus project. Physically, this was a giant matrix

3:00 PM, Memphis, Tennessee. Inventory pulled from our warehouse facility for overnight delivery.

Federal Express PartsBank® provides warehousing and distribution of your products. It's just one of many Business Logistics Services we offer.

with months written across the top, functions (or departments) down the side, and events in the boxes. There were more than 1,500 events en route from concept to customer. One person represented each function. When everyone had agreed on the overall schedule, the functional representatives had the responsibility of monitoring progress in their departments against the key events.

With Ford's key-events schedule, we have two parts of Doyle's theory: an agreement on the events that defined what the company planned to measure, and a chart that was the system for measuring.

The most colorful measuring system that I've heard of—and the easiest to read—was devised by one of consultant George Glaser's clients to track the progress of a series of software projects. A huge chart covered the walls of a war room. Each vertical line on the chart stood for a week's elapsed time. Thumbtacked to the chart were cards, each representing a chunk of work to be completed and color-coded to show whose job it was. A piece of red yarn thumbtacked to the top of the chart and weighted with a plastic coffee-cup holder at the bottom was used to track the teams' progress. As each week went by, the yarn was moved over and tacked to the next vertical line. Cards were removed as tasks were completed.

Now for Doyle's all-important third step: reading the bloody meter. Cards to the left of the red yarn showed key events that were running behind schedule. Everyone could see at a glance who was holding up the show.

Whether the meter reader arrives weekly, monthly, or bimonthly, you have to know what to do with the reading. My experience suggests that as you hit each milestone, or key event, you should report to the steering committee. The report should cover what you expected to achieve, what you did achieve, what you expected to spend, what you spent, how you define the next milestone, what you expect to produce in the next chunk, and what you estimate the next chunk will cost.

Stud poker is a good metaphor for this process. In stud poker, as in product development or any other ad hoc work, you don't know whether you've got a winner until the last card has been played. But as each card is dealt, just as a project proceeds through each phase, you buy more information on the probable success of the outcome. With each card, staying in the game gets more expensive and more risky, just as each successive phase of the project tends to get bigger and more costly than the last.

Good poker players know when to fold. Managers often don't—for several reasons. First, they don't bother to break big projects up into bite-sized chunks. Second, as the project grows, more and more people's egos and careers become invested in making sure the damned thing succeeds. Managers proceed against odds no poker player would touch because they don't see that a failure can turn into a valuable learning experience. Finally, they don't get rewarded for "the perfect mistake"—a good try that was called off for the right reasons.

A final word about implementation: It ain't over till it's over. Despite Ford's claim that "quality is job one," 80 percent of first-year Taurus and Sable buyers reported at least one glitch, according to a J. D. Power & Associates survey. Problems ranged from engine surges, stalling, electrical-system failures, and steering difficulties to a rotten-egg smell from the exhaust. Clearly the Taurus project didn't end when the first car came off the production line. This was to be expected. Any project as massive, time-sensitive, and iconoclastic as Taurus is bound to have bugs.

Good poker players know when to fold. Managers often don't.

What's remarkable to me is how Ford handled those problems. The company responded quickly to customer complaints. "We blew it; we'll fix it" was its attitude. A few years after the Taurus was unveiled, for example, Ford's service network began noticing undue wear between a certain area of the engine's piston and cylinder. The problem was traced to faulty machinery in one factory. The machines were replaced. Then Ford systematically tracked down every car that was likely to have the problem, contacted the owners, and told them to set up an appointment with their dealers to have a new engine (not a rebuilt one) installed at Ford's expense. A loaner car was provided for the inconvenience.

SUGGESTIONS
FOR GETTING RESULTS

Implementation is tough work. Make it seem crucial. Give it dignity. Hang in there.

For Executives

■ Take the emphasis off reports and put it on results. The role of the task force is to get something done, not to study it.

■ Create a management system that makes bureaucracy and adhocracy work smoothly together. Elements of the system should include the following: a widely shared view that decision-making and implementation are not separate or sequential processes, reward-systems that ennoble those who implement well, and an organization that ensures links between bureaucracy and adhocracy.

■ Insist that project teams use a systematic way of metering progress and making corrections.

For Team Leaders

■ Make plans from the outset to form multiple reporting relationships with the bureaucracy. Failure to keep the normal power structure informed is political suicide. An alienated bureaucracy will sabotage your best efforts.

■ Recognize that we-they attitudes are very likely to develop between your team and the organization. Broken loose from their current jobs and exposed to a new and broader perspective, team members can easily stray too far from the bureaucracy. Help them keep perspective.

■ Require the team to use milestones and submit regular reports. Explain to the team that its performance will be measured that way.

For Team Members

■ Start thinking the first day about implementation. Involve others in the bureaucracy: test your hypotheses with them and find out where the hotbeds of emotional resistance are.

■ Keep your boss informed about comments from others in the bureaucracy concerning the team's work.

12:10 AM, Memphis, Tennessee. Overseas shipments loaded at main hub.

With the largest all-cargo air fleet in the world, Federal Express provides global coverage for your air express shipments.

THE CONTEXT FOR VIBRANT ADHOCRACY

Structured work drives out the unstructured; that's almost a law of nature. The nature of adhocracy is both unstructured and very important, whereas the nature of bureaucracy is transfixed by structure and trivia. Because the structured organization takes precedence, opportunities get missed, crucial issues go unresolved, and efforts to change usually get nipped in the bud.

Adhocracy can flourish only in an atmosphere that discourages bureaucratic excess and uses the bureaucracy to structure team efforts. What's needed is the right environment, or what I call context. That starts with explicit statements—and implicit understandings—of the company's beliefs.

A HIGHER PURPOSE

Applied Energy Services Inc. (AES) has made an extraordinary commitment to maintaining a good context. Its belief system permeates every facet of its operation. The company, founded in 1982, sells low-cost energy. Its business is cogeneration—the production and sale of electricity and steam. So far, four plants are up and running. Each generates more than 100 megawatts, enough electrical power to serve a city of 100,000 people for a year. One more plant is nearing completion, and contracts have been signed to build five more. The company's growth has been phenomenal. Total generating potential (operating or under construction) places AES among the 100 largest utilities in the United States.

I'm especially fond of this company for a couple of reasons. First, I've known its chairman, Roger Sant, for years and have served on his board since 1984. Second, the company does business in a way that ought to make us all proud. To provide cheap energy, it burns low-cost coal and coke. The heaviest part of AES's plant investment is in the scrubbers and stacks, so that what goes back into the environment is squeaky clean—typically beating Environmental Protection Agency standards by a factor of two. The company helps solve the problem of acid rain. As for global warming concerns, AES

Dennis Bakke (left) and Roger Sant, co-founders of AES, have created a corporate environment that allows adhocracy to flourish.

put an extra $2 million into its budget for a joint venture with CARE and Guatemala to plant enough trees to absorb the carbon dioxide that its newest facility will emit.

Sant and the company's other founder, Dennis Bakke, have built AES around four basic values:

Integrity: "We try to be honest and reliable with both customers and AES's own people. We live with our agreements, even if they might hurt the company economically. Our people and our customers can rely on our word."

Fairness: "We treat customers and AES people as we would want to be treated—with respect and dignity. We believe that an ability to put ourselves in the other person's shoes is essential. We do not try to get the most out of a project at the cost of being unfair to a customer, partner, or related party."

Social benefit: "Our projects should make a positive contribution to society by lowering costs to our customers, improving product quality, increasing employment, and keeping the environment intact."

Fun: "We work because the work is fun, fulfilling, and exciting. When it stops being that way, we will change what we do."

These values drive everything the company does. They also provide the perfect context for a happy marriage of bureaucracy and adhocracy. Employees have the usual titles—chairman, chief executive, president, senior vice-president, plant manager, and so on—and the bureaucracy is built on strong functional expertise in finance, accounting, plant construction, and operations. But the evolution of the company reflects pure adhocracy.

AES started as a small band of entrepreneurs who were "maze-bright" on today's energy issues. They were able to navigate the labyrinthine channels of old bureaucracies and regulations. They quickly assimilated the financial and management know-how necessary to put together complex deals involving bankers, steam and electricity customers, and coal suppliers. Then they learned how to get the plants built on time and within budget. Finally, they acquired the engineering skills that the company needed to run the plants safely, profitably, and responsibly.

I don't think AES could have managed such an incredibly wide-ranging adhocracy without its four basic values. In the AES story lie most of the elements that make companies facile: trust and integrity; loyalty to a cause, not function; vision; humor; and an ability to cut through the trivia.

NO TRUST, NO TEAMWORK

Companies as diverse as International Business Machines Corporation, Dana Corporation, J.P. Morgan & Company, and McKinsey & Company place heavy emphasis on integrity and trust. The reason is simple: No trust, no teamwork.

Economist and Nobel prizewinner Kenneth J. Arrow believes that lack of trust severely inhibits development of any kind. He sees this as a problem in third-world cultures. People cannot work together toward a common good, Arrow says, "not only because A may betray B, but because even if A wants to trust B, he knows that B is unlikely to trust him." Arrow calls trust, integrity, and morality the invisible institutions that are essential to efficiency in any economic system.

BankAmerica Corporation's vice-chairman, Richard Rosenberg, also champions the invisible institutions. In the last decade or so, Rosenberg has helped lead some of the banking industry's most impressive turnarounds: Seattle First National Bank, Crocker Bank, and currently BankAmerica. He thinks that problems deep within the corporate culture are usually the cause of project-team failures. "The key," he says, "is to create an environment where people have respect and trust for each other." If empire-building and political intrigue permeate the company, getting a team to work for the good of the company is nearly impossible.

Apple Computer's senior vice-president of human resources, Kevin Sullivan, says that trust is a cornerstone of the infrastructure that allows projects like the New Enterprise to get off the ground: "People in most organizations develop an elaborate set of complicated behaviors that allows them to size each other up." He adds that you can eliminate much of that maypole dance by forming a culture that tells employees,

Trust, integrity, and morality are the invisible institutions that are essential to efficiency in any economic system.

"You have credibility; all you can do is lose it." This culture has become a competitive weapon at Apple. It enables the company to move more nimbly than others in the industry.

The importance of integrity and trust seems so clear, yet for most employees these corporate traits are all too elusive. A friend at Apple talks about how tough maintaining trust can be when things are constantly changing: "There is so much fluidity here—learn, act, learn, act. It has been hard for people down in the organization to trust any given direction. Management talks a lot about building trust, yet everyone from my level down can perceive a high degree of competitiveness at the executive level that suggests a lack of trust."

How do you get the rank and file to swallow talk about trust if they don't see it at the top? Fast change and the concomitant need to keep options open make even the most idealistic executives seem a little untrustworthy. As Americans, we're taught to distrust authority. Our daily papers are filled with the latest scandals in investment banking, the savings and loan industry, politics, and organized religion...even, heaven help us, in that great American institution, baseball.

McKinsey & Company, which was my employer for 21 years, has an up-or-out policy. You keep moving ahead or you're expected to leave. That sounds tough, but the administration of this policy is fairly gentle. People get second chances and lots of help when they do leave, and they often end up in jobs that are better than the ones they left. From the day I joined, however, one thing was clear: a single breach of integrity and you were out within the hour. What's more, employees at any level in the organization were empowered to go straight to the top if they saw instances of unprofessional behavior and couldn't get them resolved through their immediate supervisors.

McKinsey's basic business is making teams work effectively and reliably. Its teams were frequently drawn from offices all over the globe. Yet even those who had never met before or worked together knew they shared a common belief system—one that prized integrity, put the client first, and moved fast to correct abuse. Sant, Bakke, Arrow, Rosenberg, and Sullivan are right. The invisible institutions—trust, integrity, ethics, and morality—make our system work. Rules, policies, manuals, and laws cannot substitute. Adhocracy asks people from different fiefs to work together for the good of the whole. Trust is imperative.

US AGAINST THEM

We-they problems are the toughest obstacles to overcome for companies eager to create a context in which adhocracy and bureaucracy can peacefully coexist. Even AES, with its commitment to fairness and fun, has had to grapple with the ubiquitous problem of "us against them."

The company's Beaver Valley plant, near Pittsburgh, is a retrofit. It sits in the middle of an old World War II synthetic-rubber plant. Walls are as thick as a medieval castle's, still protecting the facility from the specter of enemy bombers. When AES bought the plant, workers' attitudes were at first as impenetrable as those walls and as rigid as Pittsburgh steel. "AES values or not," they'd say, "as soon as profits go south, you'll treat us just as badly as every other company has."

With the purchase of the Beaver Valley plant, AES had become an operating company. The board had put pressure on management to bring in more operations people and to learn more about operations themselves. One result was that all top executives at AES now spend at least one week every year in a plant, dressed in work clothes, learning and doing every job. Guided by the workers, they load coal, tend boilers, machine parts in the maintenance shop, clean fouled equipment—everything.

On comparing their impressions of work at Beaver Valley, Sant, Bakke, and others were confounded by a pattern each had repeatedly noticed. As they were trained by the operators to perform an especially inefficient, unsafe, or dirty operation, executives would ask why it was done that way. Invariably, the answer was "They make us." Who was "they"? Certainly, neither the workers nor top management wanted to keep doing things inefficiently. "They," of course, was the past— old work practices, myths, and suppositions. "They" was an army of bureaucrats who'd probably died a long time ago—

but their ghosts were still in charge at Beaver Valley.

A loose coalition (adhocracy again) led by executive vice-president Bob Hemphill moved fast to rout the spectral enemy. One day everyone in the company got a ceramic coffee cup in the mail with the words WHO IS THEY ANYWAY? baked into the glaze. Thus began a barrage of patches, lapel buttons, Post-it notes, and sheriff's badges. All had the word *they* covered by a circle with a line through it—the international don't-do-it symbol.

Later, Bakke and Hemphill distributed large cardboard posters—pictures of Sant sitting behind his desk—to every AES facility. The poster said, SEND THEY A LETTER. Postage-paid tear-off sheets were provided for mailing in suggestions and complaints. Shortly thereafter a difficult labor negotiation was disrupted by the sound of "gunfire." Four men—dressed in combat gear and carrying mock rifles—stormed the room with THEY patches sewn all over their fatigues. The guerrilla band, which called itself the Anti-They Liberation Front, turned out to be four of the company's senior officers.

By setting "they" outside the company and defusing a lot of tension with humor, AES sent a message that challenging old ways of doing things was okay. Rationalizing inefficient methods with the line "They make us do it" is no longer acceptable at Beaver Valley.

Another powerful tool for change that resulted from breaking down we-they barriers was a system designed by AES employees called the honeycomb structure. Workers have organized themselves into families. There's the turbine family, the coal-pile family, and the scrubber family. Their values, like those of any family, are communal and self-sufficient. The point is to share not just the work, but the ideas. Family members all learn each others' jobs and trade off to keep work interesting. They help each other find solutions to special problems and do routine maintenance without waiting for a specialist. Hatfields and McCoys? Not at all. Workers are encouraged to move from family to family as a means of expanding their range of skills.

The honeycomb structure has enabled AES to dramatically cut the bureaucracy and hierarchy that it had once needed to make the plants run. Nowhere in the organization are there more than three layers of management between the entry-level employee and the chief executive. Happily, the result shows up on the bottom line. In the we-they days, Beaver Valley rarely operated anywhere near capacity. It was never profitable. Today the plant is comfortably in the black, routinely runs at slightly greater than 90 percent capacity, and almost always breaks old monthly productivity records.

HOW TRIVIA KILLS TRUST

Creating the right context also means waging all-out war on mindless bureaucracy.

Several years ago I led a team working with a client that badly needed a new product to keep its historic lead in the food industry. We recommended that project teams be used for product development. I was not prepared for the company's response. Not only did the research-and-development people disagree, but they were furious. Simple rejection would have been understandable; that happens all the time when something new is suggested. But rage?

As I dug into the matter I found out what the problem was: people were being paid on a system that rewarded them for size of empire. Their salary levels and bonuses seemed to depend entirely on their standing in the bureaucracy. Every time I said "project team," they heard something else: loss of position, lower salary, no bonus.

Executives at Chevron counteract that kind of attitude by clearly making teamwork an honor. "I was being recognized as someone with potential," says Bill Crain, recalling his reaction when assigned to a team early in his career. "I got some exposure to marketing, production, and human-resource problems that I never would have gotten otherwise. The real winners on the project were the members of the team. Without participating, I could have been stuck in one function for my entire career." Crain hardly got stuck; he's now vice-president of domestic oil and gas at Chevron.

Tania Amochaev, chief executive of Natural Language Inc., a small, 250-employee software company, says that even tiny companies like hers must fight the instinct to add useless

Creating the right context means waging all-out war on mindless bureaucracy.

2:33 PM, Singapore, Malaysia. Afternoon deliveries on their way.

Federal Express delivers over 1.5 million packages
throughout the world. Every day.

Saturday, 8:52 AM, Seattle, Washington. Another workday begins.

If your work week doesn't end on Friday, Federal Express offers Saturday delivery of your important packages in the U.S.

structure. "It always shows up in the trivia," she says, and offers a particularly apt example. Natural Language set up a new policy for expense reporting. Nothing unusual about that. "Without my understanding how it happened, we had suddenly created a system whereby you had to submit every receipt, Scotch-taped on a separate sheet of paper with your expense report, or you wouldn't get paid," she says. "Clearly, somebody in accounting thought, *I'm getting a bunch of garbage here. Let's get it under control.* But it doesn't make any sense. We hire top salespeople. We tell them they will have enormous autonomy. Then we tell them to Scotch-tape receipts or we won't pay them."

Morale is undermined. Inertia sets in. Salespeople say to themselves, *I could either make three new cold calls* (tough, unstructured work), *or I could work on my in-basket.* They do the paperwork.

"You ask people, 'Is your company bureaucratic?' They say, 'Yes.' You ask for examples and it's the expense-reporting kind of example they give," says Amochaev. "It's not the serious stuff, but little things, one after another, that pile up. It gets depressing."

A company won't run without some bureaucratic procedures. But typically they're designed to suit the people administering them, not the people using them. That makes life easy for administrators. That also enervates the very people you want to be most charged up—the sales force, the service people, the folks in the plant who make or break your reputation for quality.

The trivia that Amochaev worries about grows as wantonly as weeds in a garden. It suffocates the adhocracy that can make change happen. The simplest solution is to empower people down the line to weed out the trivia. American Airlines Inc. and Hyatt Hotels Corporation, for example, have instituted say-yes programs. People at the counter can solve most customers' problems without calling a supervisor; the only time employees must call one is when they have to say no.

Hewlett-Packard, Westinghouse Electric Corporation, IBM, Boise Cascade Corporation, and others weed bureaucratic gardens through their total-quality programs. People at all levels diagram who inside the company receives or is affected by what they produce. Then they ask that "customer" about the value of the product. Natural Language's Scotch-taped expense reports would get picked up right away in a system like that.

Each of these companies has created a system for uprooting needless bureaucracy. The employees' integrity is taken for granted. Their jobs become more stimulating and more fun.

WHAT STRATEGY CAN'T DO

Strategy is part of a context that pulls people together. Woolly thinking on what is meant by strategy, however, sometimes gets in the way. Adhocracy cannot operate in a strategic vacuum; it can, however, be just the right tool to help shear the wool.

Hewlett-Packard's Richard Alberding describes the importance of strategy at his company: "We found that no matter what you do to keep the organization vibrant, including what you're calling adhocracy, it won't work very well unless your fundamental business strategy is in place. During the mid-1980s, we lost our grasp of the basic business we were in. We pushed the organization to the wall. We were choking on ad hoc organization.

"Councils, committees, task forces, and projects went on and on. They were substituting for a basic fabric that wasn't there. Instead of resolving issues, they were creating issues. Nobody could make decisions. I don't think it was until about 1987 that we broke the code on that."

Here's the strategy statement the company came up with: "Hewlett-Packard provides the tools to harness the power of information. Instruments to make precise measurements. A range of powerful computers and peripheral products to help analyze, manage, and store information. Graphics and printing capabilities to make it visible. Networking and software to link it all together. These capabilities—combined with a commitment to quality, customer satisfaction, and a strong global presence—give HP a solid foundation for future innovation and growth."

Simple, isn't it? But strategic? Where's the drama, the vision? People down the line at Hewlett-Packard might claim that they still don't have a strategy that gives them the sense of direction they would like to receive from management.

The confounding problem is that we need strategy, but we expect far too much from it. Unfortunately, for most people the word *strategy* conjures up images of brilliant military leaders moving pieces on table-sized maps, or double agents infiltrating the KGB. Well, in real life, intricate plans don't work; Murphy's law gets them every time.

The right strategy acknowledges that our vision of the future will never be crystal clear. Broad, commonsense statements about the long term, like Hewlett-Packard's, are usually the best we can do. This is an unsettling message for people down the line, who are looking for more clarity. But the best strategy combines a coherent general sense of direction with a deep understanding of the business and an organizational form that allows a company to react quickly to new opportunity.

Moreover, the best strategy is process; it is not a plan. One of the most important parts of the process is the ability to identify and focus on a few key issues each year. Having identified those issues, what do you do? Organize a team, of course, to turn them into opportunities. So how can the reverse also be true—how can the ad hoc approach help to develop strategy and vision?

AES is grappling with some tough questions about its future direction right now. To help sort them out, five executives were asked to explore five radically different options. They each threw together a small team, studied the option in depth, then presented their findings to the board of directors. Rarely have I seen better work on strategy. The board was recognizing real options. Usually just one option, the chief executive's favorite, is given full review, followed by a cursory analysis of several straw men. In this case, none of the five options was clearly the best. In fact, one board member said, only half in jest, "Let's do them all." But that was exactly the point. The company needed the board's best thinking and that was the only way to get it.

In real life, intricate plans don't work. Murphy's law gets them every time.

THE PYGMALION EFFECT

Adhocracy works where people expect it to work. The late Stanford University philosophy professor Philip H. Rhinelander said that none of us can change the laws of physics and chemistry by thinking about them. But we can change our own behavior by thinking about it. This is the power of self-fulfilling prophecy, the Pygmalion effect. People do better if they are expected to do better, and worse if they are expected to do worse.

One quality that distinguishes AES and HP from other organizations that I've known well over the years is that these companies have a can-do attitude. When Bob Swanson started Genentech, his favorite phrase was "Make it happen!" He believed his group could do what many others considered impossible. The team at AES behaves the same way. So do the folks at Bridge Housing Corporation. By and large they've been right. Can-do attitudes help the cause of change generally and project teams specifically.

SUGGESTIONS FOR CREATING THE RIGHT CONTEXT

Adhocracy can flourish only if the context is right. There is much that you can do in your organization to help establish an easy balance between bureaucracy and adhocracy.

For Executives

■ Make room for adhocracy. Take as much unnecessary structure as possible out of bureaucracy. Adopt programs like total quality that force the design of procedure around users. Empower everyone to tell you what seems dumb.

■ Fight we-they attitudes. Over time, one of the most powerful ways to do this is to throw people together on teams. Ford and other American manufacturers have found that there's no better way to break down old labor-management barriers than by sending a team of union leaders, workers, and managers to Japan to see firsthand just what world-class manufacturing looks like.

■ Write down the basic values that ought to drive the company. Build an organization that celebrates trust, integrity, morality, and ethics. Be quick to dismiss people for breaches of those values, and let other employees know your reasoning. Empower and encourage people to challenge authority when it forces unethical behavior. Be less quick to dismiss people for errors in business judgment; treat these as investments in learning.

■ Keep perspective on strategy and vision. What's needed are simple statements that help organizations and their employees to make sense of the world and focus on what's important.

For Team Leaders and Members

■ You'll be the first to see the trivia. Catalog it and help the people you work with to get rid of it, even if that's not part of your main assignment.

■ What do you do if asked to serve on a team in which trust doesn't exist? You have three options, none of them easy. First, go through the motions; adhocracy won't accomplish much, but you'll be safe. Second, get off; again, adhocracy won't accomplish much, but you will not have wasted your time. Finally, make waves; that is the greatest test of your loyalty to the organization and it to you.

■ Being picked for project work is an honor in many organizations. Treat it as an opportunity to learn and grow.

The main function of organizations is not to make a profit. It's to fulfill a social purpose—to give us goods and services that we need or want, to provide jobs, to enhance the quality of life. Profit, or in the case of nonprofit organizations, breaking even, is like health or breathing. They're not why you exist, but you wouldn't survive long without them. The healthier and more profitable a business, the better it can fulfill its main social purpose. One reinforces the other. That's what makes capitalism efficient.

But capitalism has a nasty downside. Economist Joseph Schumpeter called it creative destruction. The fit survive and the newly fit drive out the old. In dealing with change, American companies are more destructive and less creative than they need to be. We are transfixed by the quarterly bottom line and don't invest in change. We're lazy; for too long we rested on a hammock supported by industrial regulation on one side and lack of keen global competition on the other. We're unimaginative; we try to deal with change primarily through the very mechanism that resists change: bureaucracy.

We talk today as if our main problem is rapid change, per se. I don't buy that. The problem is our inability to take change in stride. The problem is that we seemingly have no other tool than Schumpeter's creative destruction.

The best means we have for dealing gracefully with change is well-managed adhocracy. It is not the only means, but I believe it's the most powerful. Like change, the idea of adhocracy is not new. But the idea that adhocracy can and should be managed in tandem with bureaucracy is new. We desperately need management theory and practice that codifies this proposition. The ideas presented here, I hope, provide the right start.

Anytime, any place, in the air and on the ground, Federal Express is working to meet the needs of business throughout the world.

Additional Copies

To order additional copies of *Adhocracy: The Power
to Change* for friends or colleagues, please write to
The Larger Agenda Series, Whittle Direct Books,
505 Market St., Knoxville, Tenn. 37902. Please
include the recipient's name, mailing address,
and, where applicable, title, company name,
and type of business.

For a single copy, please enclose a check for $11.95
payable to The Larger Agenda Series. When
ordering 10 or more books, enclose $9.95 for
each; for orders of 50 or more books, enclose
$7.95 for each. If you wish to place an order by
phone, call 800-284-1956.

Also available, at the same prices, are copies of
the previous book in The Larger Agenda Series:
The Trouble With Money by William Greider.

Please allow two weeks for delivery.
Tennessee residents must add 7¾ percent sales tax.

119430

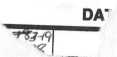

DA